Bought for 50p in Matlock from a second-hand
Tony 20-1-2015 — I knew Charlie very well in

The Complete Sport Parachuting Guide

Charles Shea-Simonds

In the same series:

The Complete Cycle Sport Guide
The Complete Hang Gliding Guide
The Complete Sailing Guide
The Complete Soaring Guide
The Complete Windsurfing Guide

The Complete
SPORT PARACHUTING
Guide

Charles
Shea-Simonds

photography by
Simon Ward

A & C Black
London

First published 1986 by
A & C Black (Publishers) Ltd
35 Bedford Row
London WC1R 4JH

Shea-Simonds, Charles
 The complete sport parachuting guide.
 1. Parachuting
 I. Title
 797.5'6   GV770

 ISBN 0-7136-5562-3

Typeset by August Filmsetting, St Helens.
Printed and bound in Great Britain by
Hazell Watson & Viney Ltd, Aylesbury, Bucks.

Design: Janet Simmonett

Photographic credits

All photographs by Simon Ward, except the
following:
Tony Dale: p. 39
Charles Shea-Simonds: pp. 10 (left), 31, 46,
 50, 54, 70, 74, 75 (bottom), 78, 86, 87, 107,
 115, 119, 130

Acknowledgements
My sincere thanks are due to all who have
made this book possible, particularly: the
Council of the British Parachute Association
and its Chairman, Jim Crocker; Charles Port,
Tony Butler, John Hitchen and Suzie Allen at
the BPA Office; the Army Parachute
Association, especially Gerry O'Hara, Tony
Rose and his predecessor, John Laing, and
Jackie Smith; Simon Ward (with assistance
from Olympus Cameras & Fuji Film) for his
excellent photographs; that 'wise old
pelican', trusted friend and co-BPA Vice
President, John Meacock, for years of expert
advice; and, finally, to my Julie for her
encouragement and typing of the text.

Contents

The build-up of a 90-way freefall formation.

1. What is sport parachuting?

The word 'parachute' is attributed to a French professor of physics and chemistry, Sebastian Le Normand, and literally means 'break fall', which is exactly what happened when he descended safely from the tower of Montpellier observatory, France, on 26 December 1783. His crude parachute was only fourteen feet in diameter but it was sufficient to break his fall and prevent injury.

Leonardo da Vinci had sketched the design of a rigid parachute in 1495 but, of course, lacked a flying machine from which to test it. Ballooning provided the first practical lift to altitude and it was from a hot air balloon on 22 October 1797 2,500′ over Park Monceau in Paris that André Jacques Garnerin made the first proper parachute descent from a flying machine. Garnerin in a sense was also the first sport parachutist as there was little other practical use for the parachute in those days other than for exhibitions—which is, of course, how so much of early aviation developed.

It needed the First World War to provide a practical use for the parachute as a means of saving life. Initially it was used by crews of observation balloons who, if their balloons were destroyed by enemy fire, leapt over the side whereupon a line attached firmly to the balloon basket deployed the life saving emergency parachute. This 'static line' system of parachute canopy deployment was also used for emergency descents from aeroplanes during the latter days of the War, but there was always the danger of the static line and deploying parachute becoming entangled with the stricken aeroplane. There was clearly a need for the pilot to be able to fall clear of the aeroplane before manually initiating canopy deployment. However, it was not until after the War that the first 'freefall' parachute descent was made. McCook Field, Ohio, was the US Army airfield used for testing parachute equipment and it was here on 28 April 1919 that Leslie Irvin made the first freefall descent from a DH9 aeroplane flown by fellow pioneer, Floyd Smith, the equipment's designer. The success of this descent opened the door to the rapid development of the parachute along three distinct avenues.

First was the very reason the McCook Field programme was initiated—that of saving a pilot's life in an emergency situation. In 1922 a Lt. Harris became the first pilot, having abandoned a disabled aeroplane, to save his life using a parachute: he was the first of thousands of pilots and aircrew who have reason to be grateful for the parachute.

Second was the development of the parachute as a means of delivering soldiers and their equipment into battle. Pioneered in the Soviet Union during the 1930s, the Second World War saw whole divisions deployed into battle in this way and even now parachute forces are the elite of powerful military nations.

Third was the development of the sport of parachuting—the subject of this book. Because of its quasi-military nature sport parachuting developed in the first instance alongside the development of military parachuting in the Soviet Union in the 1930s; but it was not until after the Second World War that sport parachuting really gained momentum. Before any activity can be truly called a sport, there must be a strong competitive element and in 1951 five nations met in Yugoslavia for a parachuting competition which was, in essence, the first World Championships. It was not until the second World Championships were held at St Yan in France in 1954 that the Fédération Aéronautique Internationale, the international governing body of aviation sport, recognised parachuting as a sport.

Thus in 40 years sport parachuting has developed into a highly technological and skilful recreational activity that can have enormous appeal for people of all ages. The governing body of parachuting within the United Kingdom is the British Parachute Association and is based in Leicester. It is responsible both to the Sports Council and to the Civil Aviation Authority for the sport's safe conduct and control. It also has a link through the Royal Aero club of the United Kingdom to the Fédération Aéronautique Internationale whose headquarters are in Paris and which looks after the interests of sporting aviation throughout the world.

An historic moment in parachuting history. Leslie Irvin makes the first ever freefall parachute jump over McCook Field, Ohio, on 28 April 1919.

2. Before you jump

Before you jump it is worth discovering more about the various organisations which are concerned with sport parachuting. For example, the British Parachute Association (Kimberley House, 47 Vaughan Way, Leicester LE1 4SG) controls sport parachuting in Great Britain and is thus responsible to the Civil Aviation Authority for all aspects of the sport. The BPA employs a full-time National Coach and Safety Officer whose responsibilities are self-explanatory. The BPA also has a Safety and Training Committee which is made up of the country's most experienced instructors. Its function is to advise on all matters of training and safety and to revise and amend the *BPA Operations Manual* as necessary. The BPA appoints qualified instructors and ensures that they control sport parachuting in accordance with its *Operations Manual*. The BPA is responsible, too, for the organisation of National Parachute Championships, the selection of the National Team and its training for the World Championships and other international events. The Association publishes its own bi-monthly magazine, *Sport Parachutist*, which provides articles and photographs on all aspects of the sport, and is a means of communicating up-to-date information to its members.

It is required by law that all sport parachutists are covered by insurance for third party liability, and to this end the BPA covers its members to the sum of £500,000. This policy is held in the BPA offices, and the service is a most useful one: provided you are parachuting in accordance with the regulations laid down in its *Operations Manual*, the BPA will be financially responsible for damage to property or persons that you might cause as a direct result of a parachute descent. The Association also maintains an up-to-date register of active parachute clubs throughout the country and thus you can be put in touch with the club nearest to where you live by contacting the Secretary General at the address given above. When you first arrive at your club and you sign up the necessary club documentation forms you will automatically be made a provisional member of the British Parachute Association and this will cover you for your first six parachute descents. If you wish to continue with the sport you can up-rate your provisional membership to a permanent one and, therefore, for a nominal annual subscription you are benefitted in the following three basic ways: (1) you are given world-wide third party insurance cover up to £500,000; (2) you receive the magazine, *Sport Parachutist*, six

times a year; and most important of all (3) you receive the services of an association which is constantly striving to better the sport and ensure your safety in parachuting.

Another organisation which you should know about is the Royal Aero Club. All aviation sports are represented at the Royal Aero Club and it, in turn, acts as a co-ordinating link with the FAI (the International Aviation Federation) whose headquarters are in Paris. The FAI is the international controlling body of all aviation sports and each sport is represented by its own committee, whether it be for ballooning, aero-modelling, helicopters, gliders, hang-gliders or parachuting. The FAI essentially controls all the international rules for competitive parachuting and records.

Once you have joined your local parachute club you will be required either to consult your local doctor for a parachuting medical (essential if you are over 40 years of age) or, in some cases, to sign a simple medical declaration. Whichever, you should be physically fit before you think about making a parachute descent. It is worth quoting from the BPA Medical Certificate: 'Parachutists make descents from unpressurized aircraft at heights of between 2,000′ and 12,000′ above sea level without using oxygen. They must open their parachutes at

Two 28' flat circular canopies.

An early 5-cell ram-air canopy—the Strato Star.

a safe height above the ground and be prepared to take emergency action if their main parachute fails to open correctly. They should, therefore, be of an emotionally stable type. During landing there are forces to be absorbed by the body approximately equivalent to jumping from a platform $4\frac{1}{2}$ ft from the ground. Depending on the weight of the parachutist, weather conditions and other factors, a landing force may be greater than this equivalent. The examinee must be in good general health and possess a sound musculo-skeletal system. The lower limbs usually accept the brunt of the landing force. The minimum visual acuity of both eyes with or without glasses which is acceptable is 6/12 and the candidate must not be red/green colour blind. Hearing must be normal and it should be remembered that chronic sinusitis or otitis media is not compatible with rapid changes of air pressure that will occur during the descent. The presence of any of the following conditions make a person unfit to parachute: diabetes and other glandular disfunction, epilepsy, fainting attacks or a history of psychiatric disorder. Any history of skull fracture, concussion or brain damage should be assessed most carefully, for in the course of landing the head may strike the ground with force and brain damage tends to be cumulative. In cases of doubt a normal EEG pattern must be present.'

In Britain there are one or two other documents that you will come across during your early parachuting days, the first of which is the BPA Training Card. This card records all aspects of your training up to and including your first parachute descent. From then on you will be given what is called a BPA Category Card. It shows each

of the 10 categories of the sport parachutist as outlined in a later chapter, and it will be dated and signed by your instructor when you reach the standard of each category. Once you have made your first two or three descents and have decided that you are going to continue with the sport, you are obliged to record all your parachute descents in a log book. Log books may be obtained from the BPA office and they contain spaces for normally 200 descents, and record the following details of descents: number, date and time, dropping zone, aircraft type, qualified parachutist or pilot signature and certificate/licence number, back-chute type, altitude, delay in seconds, manoeuvres, distance from target, wind in mph, and remarks. Every descent should be recorded in detail as soon as possible after it is made because you will find that during your later progression you are able to qualify for certain certificates issued by the BPA on behalf of the International Aviation Federation. This certificate is known as an FAI Parachutist's Certificate. It is an internationally recognised certificate of agreed parachuting standards; thus if you wish to parachute abroad, this certificate is a most useful document to be able to produce. The standards required are as follows:

Certificate A Category 3 and 10 jumps.

Certificate B Category 5 and 25 jumps to include 10 jumps landing within 50 metres of the target.

Certificate C Category 8 and 50 jumps to include 20 jumps landing within 20 metres of the target.

Certificate D Category 10 and 200 jumps to include 20 jumps landing within 15 metres of the target.

The form must be countersigned by a BPA Instructor to show that you have reached the required standard for the certificate for which you are applying.

The BPA is also responsible for issuing FAI Parachute Competitors' Licences which you will require later if you wish to compete in national or international parachuting championships. Application forms as for normal FAI certificates are available from the BPA office and are completed in much the same way as that for a standard FAI certificate.

Once you have bought your own parachute you must keep a parachute log card to record when you pack the parachute and carry out any modifications or repairs. Following from this is a packing certificate which will be granted to you when your instructor considers that you are competent to pack parachutes without supervision.

3. Equipment

Parachutes

Sport parachutists, whatever their experience, are required to be equipped with two parachutes attached to a common harness. These two are the 'main' parachute, which it is hoped will function correctly on every descent, and the 'reserve' or emergency parachute to be used should the main malfunction. These two parachutes are packed in two separate containers which may be positioned in one of two ways: either 'fore and aft' with the main parachute worn on the back and with the reserve on the front; or the 'tandem system' with the main container located below the reserve on the back. Initially, you are likely to use the fore and aft system before progressing to the tandem system. The reason for this is that in the early student days it is easier to handle the deployment of the reserve parachute when you can see it mounted across your stomach, although there are student tandem systems available.

The main parachute will be one of two distinct types. As a student you will almost certainly start parachuting using a conventionally shaped round parachute before progressing at some later stage to a high performance square or 'ram-

The 'G.Q. Aeroconical' student main canopy.

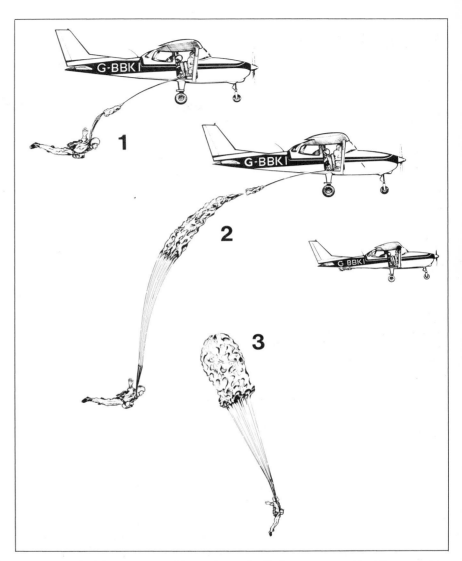

air' parachute. The same principle applies to the reserve parachute, with both round and square types in use. Deployment of the main parachute follows a 'line-first sequence' while that of a round reserve follows a 'canopy-first' sequence—the difference will be clear in due course.

Taking main canopy deployment first, it is logical to consider that of the static-line initiated sequence as this is almost certainly what you will be using for your first descent. The 15-ft long, 5,000 lb breaking strain nylon static line has one end attached by a snap-hook to a strong point in the aeroplane. The other end passes through elastic pack closure loops before routeing inside the container and being attached to the deployment bag in which is packed the canopy itself.

Parachute canopies

All sport parachute canopies, round or square, are manufactured from nylon and, while this is enormously strong, all canopies are packed with some form of deployment device which is designed to decelerate the opening to an acceptable level, both for the canopy itself and for the human frame. In the case of the static line canopy, which will always be of the round variety, the deployment device is a bag to which is attached the other end of the static line. The canopy,

constructed with a system of 'gores' and 'panels', is packed neatly within the bag which is closed with a flap called the 'mouth-lock'. The mouth-lock is in turn held in place with the stowage of the canopy lines (called 'suspension' or 'rigging' lines) in

elastic loops preventing the opening of the bag. The bag is packed in the main container with the side, top and bottom flaps kept closed by the static line. The lines are attached to the harness by way of metal 'connector links', heavy webbing

A view of the 'GQ Aeroconical' student canopy showing the drive and steering vents.

down the bulk of the overall system.

The parachute canopy itself is made of nylon and the amount of air the material will allow to pass through is related to the 'porosity' of the canopy. A low porosity canopy, affectionately called a 'Lo-Po', allows less air to pass through it than does a high porosity canopy. A normal 28-ft, flat, circular canopy has 28 'gores', a gore being the wedge-shaped part of the canopy between each rigging line. In turn

straps or 'risers' and the canopy release system, normally of the 'Capewell' variety.

The design of the sleeve-deployed parachute is slightly different. From the top, the 'pilot-chute' (sometimes called the 'extractor' or 'drogue') is the small parachute that pulls the rest of the parachute from the pack. It has a strong spring built into it which ejects the pilot-chute clear of your back when the pack is opened. This system is the one that you are likely to use for your first freefall descent. The 'bridle line' is a strong nylon cord (normally of about 1,000 lb breaking strain) that connects the pilot-chute to the sleeve, and the sleeve is attached to the apex of the parachute by the 'sleeve retaining line'. The 'apex' of the parachute is the whole of the top where the rigging lines can also be seen. The

'deployment sleeve' is a long sock-like device which contains the parachute canopy to ensure that the rigging lines have been deployed before the canopy starts to inflate and that the opening is relatively gradual, thus reducing the shock in the same way as with the static-line operated bag-deployed parachute. The sleeve is normally made of a strong linen fabric so that when it slides off the canopy during deployment the nylon is not burnt through friction. At the bottom of the sleeve is a flap of material with a hole in each corner. This is the mouth-lock which is the same as the one at the bottom of the bag on the static-line system. The alternative to the sleeve is a shortened version called the 'diaper', which in principle is exactly the same but it leaves the top part of the canopy exposed and cuts

The first-timer ready to go, complete with static-line main and chest-mounted reserve assembly.

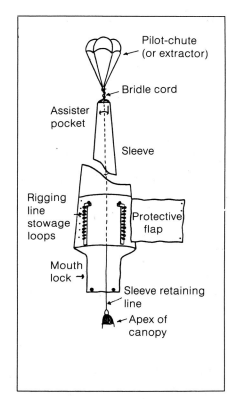

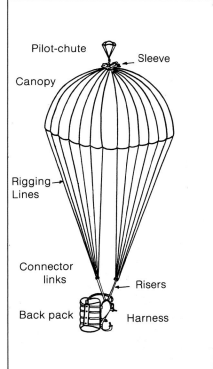

The parts of the parachute.

The 28 ft flat circular canopy modified to a double 'L'.
Note: Lines 1–7 go to the left rear riser
Lines 8–14 go to the left front riser
Lines 15–21 go to the right front riser
Lines 22–28 go to the right rear riser
The two steering lines are attached to lines 6 and 23 respectively.

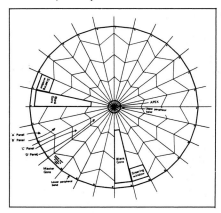

each gore is divided into four panels from the bottom lettered (a), (b), (c) and (d). You will notice from the diagram opposite that the seams between each panel are at a different angle on adjacent gores; this gives added strength to the manufacture of the canopy which in this case is called 'bias construction'. Each gore can easily be identified by a number (1–28) which is found in the bottom right-hand corner. This number also identifies the rigging line. Around the apex of the canopy (at the top) is a heavy band of material known as the 'upper peripheral band', and

the heavy band around the bottom of the canopy is known as the 'lower peripheral band'. The rigging lines or suspension lines are those which join the canopy to the harness. Although there appear to be 28 lines this is not actually so, since there are in fact 14 whole lines which run continuously from the harness, up through the canopy, over the apex, down through the canopy again to the opposite side and back to the harness. Each rigging line, again made of nylon, has a breaking strain of about 500 lb, and 28 times 500 lb adds up to a lot of breaking strain!

The harness
The harness is made of the same type of nylon webbing as the risers, i.e. with a breaking strain of some 6,500 lb. The harness should be as tight as possible without being uncomfortable. You will normally find seven points of adjustment on the harness:
○ the two back adjustments
○ the two body adjustments
○ the two leg straps
○ the chest strap.
Sewn around the harness just below one of the canopy releases you will find the ripcord pocket. This is an elastic-sided nylon pocket which

houses the ripcord handle when the parachute is packed. From the top of the ripcord pocket the ripcord housing runs to the top flap of the pack. This housing is a flexible metal cover through which the ripcord runs. The ripcord is a cable of braded stainless steel, with a handle on one end and a series of pins on the other which actually lock the pack closed. The pack is that part of the parachute which houses the canopy, sleeve and rigging lines together on your back. It will normally have a small top and bottom flap, each with a nylon loop attached and two large side flaps. The flap on one side will have a grommet at the top, then a nylon loop and another grommet at the bottom. The other flap has a stiffened wide edge with a line of three grommets running down it. The nylon loops will pass through the grommets and in turn the ripcord pins will pass through these loops and hold the container closed. The reserve parachute will be attached to the harness by two clips locating on two heavy-duty D-rings which are sewn in as an integral part of the harness. The sides of the reserve are held in place by two tie-down straps: these are attached to another D-ring on the main parachute harness.

Student freefall assembly with capewell canopy releases, altimeter and FXC 12000 A.O.D.

Canopy deployment sequence.

Canopy deployment

There are two basic different types of canopy deployment. The freefall (sleeved canopy) deployment is of the 'line-first' variety which, as the name implies, starts with the suspension lines being pulled out full length before the canopy fills with air. (Conversely, the reserve canopy deployment is of the less sophisticated canopy-first type, with the canopy filling with air which in turn pulls out the lines. It is, by its very nature, a faster deployment and is exactly what one requires in an emergency situation.) When the ripcord handle is pulled, the pins are withdrawn from the nylon loops and this allows the sides of the pack to open. In fact the sides are pushed open by the spring-loaded pilot-chute which is stowed inside the container. The instant the pack opens the pilot-chute is ejected from it by means of the spring inside, which in turn pulls the sleeve away from the pack—the pilot-chute, of course, having deployed in the flow of air past the body. When the sleeve is clear of the pack the rigging lines start to deploy from the elastic bands or retaining bands at its base. The pilot-chute is still pulling the sleeve and additional lift is given by two pockets sewn on either side of it at the top. The air flow now enters the bottom of the canopy and this air flow forces the sleeve from the last few feet. The

canopy now deploys from the top downwards until the air flow has opened it completely. This whole sequence will take about 2–3 seconds.

Reserve parachute

The reserve parachute is in essence very much simpler. Initially you are likely to use a flat, circular, 24-ft canopy. However, reserve canopies specially designed for the sport are now becoming more popular and they vary slightly in design and are normally 26 ft in diameter. The modern reserve canopies have the two advantages of a low rate of descent combined with manoeuvrability. The standard 24-ft canopy has little control and is thus designed purely as a life-saver. The parts of the reserve parachute are very much the same as in the main. The 24-ft reserve canopy has 24 gores and thus 24 rigging lines (or 12 complete lines running from connector link to opposite connector link). Some reserve parachutes have short risers (about

17

Canopy deployment.

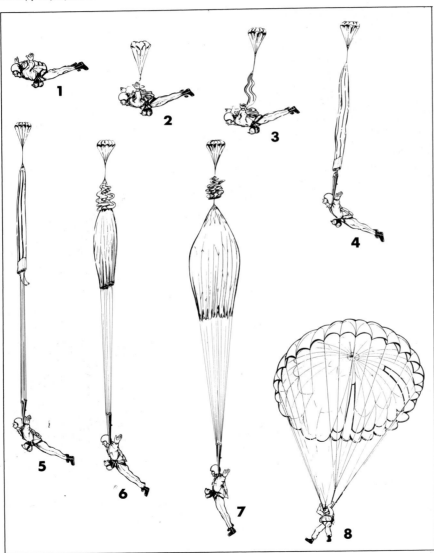

12 inches long) which terminate in two hooks, and on others the rigging lines go directly to the two hooks. These two hooks are used to attach the reserve to the D-rings on the main harness and should always be joined together by a length, about 10 inches, of 6,500 lb nylon webbing (or the equivalent length and strength in 500 lb cord looped continuously between them). The reason for the hooks being joined is that in the unlikely event of one hook becoming undone, the reserve canopy will remain inflated and attached to the main harness by the other hook on its own.

The reserve parachute has no sleeve to ensure that the opening, when required, is as fast as possible. The reserve pack has much in common with its main counterpart. There are four flaps that close around the packed canopy and are held together with the ripcord pins inserted through the loops, which in turn protrude through the grommets. With the absence of a sleeve the rigging lines are stowed in elastic bands attached to webb loops in the pack tray. The reserve is operated by pulling the ripcord handle (normally located in a pocket on the top of the pack); this releases the loops from the grommets and the pack opening bands pull the flaps open, thus allowing the canopy to deploy. The sequence here is opposite to

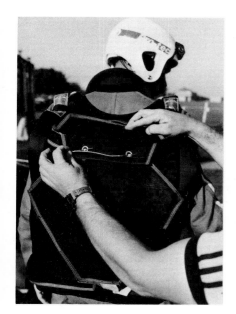

Left Reserve container pin check (on a tandem assembly).

Right The static line assembly.

container from which the lines start to deploy. Once the lines are fully deployed the bag mouthlock opens and the canopy is pulled out. An apex tie (normally of 100 lb breaking strain) between the apex of the canopy and the loop on the inside of the top of the bag prevents the canopy leaving the bag in an uncontrolled bundle; the whole sequence takes place in about 2 seconds with the canopy deploying almost instantaneously.

Personal equipment

A one-piece overall or flying suit is desirable, firstly to prevent any

the main canopy deployment as the canopy pays out before the rigging lines; the reserve canopy therefore opens considerably quicker than does the main. The last part of the reserve parachute is the tie-down; this is a webb strap with a hook on each end and a buckle to adjust its length. Each snap-hook is hooked to the tie-down D-rings at the base of the main pack. When pulled up tightly the tie-down keeps the reserve flush with the body.

In the case of the bag static line system already described the deployment is very simple to understand. When you fall away from the aircraft, your body weight breaks the tie holding the pack closed or pulls the static line from

the nylon loops (depending which system is used), and the static line pulls the bagged canopy from the

Static line bag deployment—faults: head down, not enough arch, legs out of control.

pieces of material flapping loosely as a result of wearing two or more articles of clothing, and secondly to save undue wear on your normal clothing which might come about through constant practice of parachute landings and moving around in the somewhat cramped and sometimes dirty interiors of light aircraft. Of course, one can buy a proper jump-suit designed for the job but, as with much of the equipment to be mentioned, there is little point in spending unnecessarily large sums of money until you are certain you are going to carry on with the sport.

Until you qualify further, for example for a BPA C Certificate, it is advisable you wear white (either overalls or a jump suit); the reason for this is that it enables your instructor to observe distinctly your parachuting performance. Once you have gained a C Certificate you may wear a jump suit of any colour, but bright colours are advised to avoid the possibility of mid-air collisions.

The next item is a helmet. Any peakless motorcycle helmet approved by the British Standards Institute or equivalent foreign organisation is suitable. The only exception to this are those helmets approved by the Safety and Training Committee of the British Parachute Association. A word of warning here, however, seems relevant. You will be wearing a helmet to protect your head, firstly when leaving the aircraft, secondly in freefall (in the unlikely event of someone careering into you) and thirdly during the landing itself. No helmet will last indefinitely and a parachutist's helmet will tend to take more of a bashing than one worn by a motor-cyclist, who would probably replace it anyway if it took a severe knock. I, therefore, believe that once you have taken up the sport a really good helmet is a sensible buy; but, of course, it's *your* head!

The next two items of personal equipment are very straightforward. First of all a pair of goggles to stop unnecessary bits of grit, etc., getting into your eyes and causing problems with your vision when you most need it; and secondly, a pair of gloves, particularly when the weather is cold. There are no hard and fast rules about either of these pieces of equipment and only personal experimentation will produce the best result, but at first follow your instructor's advice.

Finally the last two items will initially be supplied by your club as they are both relatively expensive. The first of these is an altimeter—obviously to tell you your height above the ground, and there are a number of types available on the market. An alternative to an altimeter is an audio-warning device which will set off a tone when a certain altitude above the ground is reached. Both these pieces of equipment are barometrically operated. Also barometrically operated is the automatic opening device which many clubs use on reserve parachutes. There are one or two different types on the market and you may well consider it a wise investment when you purchase your own equipment. All the pieces of equipment described above, including the parachutes themselves, will be provided in the first instance by your parachute club. Please do not consider buying any equipment until you have had a chance to see what is available and follow the advice of those who guide you through the early days in the sport.

4. The basic training programme

Before you start your basic training it is worth bearing the following in mind. Firstly, you must be completely resolved that you are going to pay attention to every part of your parachute training. Sport parachuting is not essentially a hazardous activity but it may be if certain aspects of the training are either ignored or left out. It is, therefore, important that you don't miss anything.

Secondly, you should also be physically fit. This has already been mentioned but it is worth considering that apart from basic physical fitness you must be alert and determined. This does not mean that you have to be a superman or superwoman, only that a little common sense is required; for instance a gentle jog around the airfield never hurt anyone and it can help a great deal. Always get a good night's sleep and keep off the alcohol: when you are actually parachuting it is forbidden to consume alcohol until you have carried out your last parachute jump of the day. (It is also important that you avoid a drinking session during the evening before parachuting the following day. Alcohol dims your mental processes and slows your reactions so it is equally important to lay off during your ground training.) Once you start parachuting you should not jump unless you feel fit in every way;

even the common cold has its dangers due to the changes in atmospheric pressure to which you will be subjected. And if you are in any way taking prescription drugs, check with your doctor before you parachute.

Finally, it's worth stressing that you must have an enquiring mind. If anything your instructor tells you is not absolutely crystal clear, then don't be afraid to ask him and make sure he runs through it all again. He may very well tell you to do something but he may not give you the reason for it—make sure you ask him. Watch other parachutists and learn from their mistakes. Never be afraid to grill the really experienced parachutist for additional knowledge. Read everything you can on the subject and study all available photographs. Much of the practical side of your ground training you can practise away from your club—don't restrict your training to the airfield alone. In Britain your initial ground training will be carried out in accordance with the BPA minimum ground training programme, which is as follows:

1 Orientation   30 minutes
a Documentation (check BPA membership, insurance, medical certificate, BPA classification card, etc.)

Main container pin check (on a tandem assemby).

b Outline of training syllabus.
c Routine safety instructions to be observed with aircraft (crossing runways, etc.)
d Orientation flight (if desired).

2 Introduction   30 minutes
a Safety regulations.
b Equipment and dress.
c Introduction to aircraft to be used in training.
d Wind drift determination.
e Exit technique (stability).
f Emergency procedures.
g Canopy handling.
h Landing techniques.
i Parachute packing.

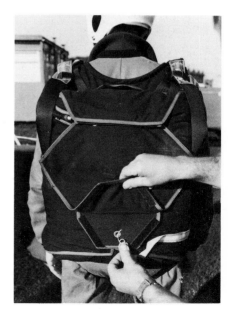

Pulling the ripcord: look and reach for the ripcord handle, then 'pull' and recover.

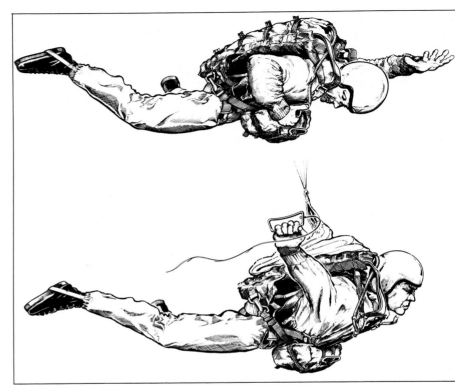

3 Familiarisation with parachutes 90 minutes
a The anatomy of the main assembly.
b The anatomy of the reserve assembly.
c The functioning of main and reserve parachutes.
d Parachute fitting.
e Pre-planning a parachute descent.
f Equipment-checking procedure.

4 Familiarisation with aircraft 30 minutes
a Safety checks.
b Procedures for entering and exiting with particular reference to guarding reserve parachutes.
c Static line procedure.
d Signals and words of command in the air.

5 Aircraft exits 60 minutes
a Preparatory commands and signals and actions.
b Move into exit position.
c Position after exit (stable position).
d Counting, count follow-through and, later, dummy ripcord pulls (DRCP).

6 Emergency procedures 90 minutes
a Verbal count—static line.
b Verbal count—freefall:
(1) Count prior to ripcord pull.
(2) Count after ripcord pull.

c Check of main canopy immediately after opening.
d Recognition of malfunctions.
e Corrective actions:
(1) Total malfunction.
(2) Partial malfunctions (stable and spinning).
f Drill period using suspended harness.

7 Canopy handling 60 minutes
(Using suspended harness if possible)
a Check canopy.
b Orientation with ground:
(1) Grasp toggles.
(2) Ascertain location over ground, target and drift.
(3) Work to wind line (zigzag method, etc. to obtain).
(4) Check vertical angle of descent (hold or run).
(5) Avoidance of obstacles (do not become intent on target).
(6) Suspended harness drill period.
c Prepare to land:
(1) Altitude to adopt landing position: approx. 150 ft (8–10 seconds).
(2) Body position, face into wind.

The jumper's view of a flat circular 28' canopy with 'double L' modification. (The jumper is facing towards the left of the photograph.)

(3) Obeying ground instructions if loudspeaker equipment is available.

8 Parachute landing falls 90 minutes
a Types:
   (1) Normal (front, back, side).
   (2) Tree.
   (3) Power line.
   (4) Water.
b Five (5) points of body contact.
c Recovery from drag:
   (1) Hit, roll, recover, run.
   (2) Pulling lines.
   (3) Capewell.

9 Field rolling the parachute 30 minutes
a Chain lines.
b Sleeve over canopy.
c Close one side flat with pack-opening bands.
d Secure all equipment and move to packing area.

10 Dropping zone duties 30 minutes
a Responsibility.
b Control.
c Rotation of personnel.

11 Parachute packing instruction (backpacks only) 3 hours

12 Testing—all phases 60 minutes

A student freefall assembly prior to pilot-chute stowage and pack closure.

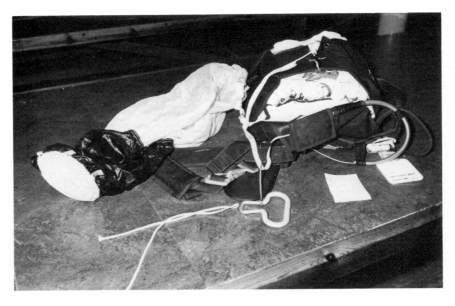

Summary

Subject	Duration (hours)
1 Orientation	$\frac{1}{2}$
2 Introduction	$\frac{1}{2}$
3 Familiarisation with parachutes	$1\frac{1}{2}$
4 Familiarisation with aircraft	$\frac{1}{2}$
5 Aircraft exits	1
6 Emergency procedures	$1\frac{1}{2}$
7 Canopy handling	1
8 Parachute landing falls	$1\frac{1}{2}$
9 Field rolling the parachute	$\frac{1}{2}$
10 Dropping zone duties	$\frac{1}{2}$
11 Parachute packing instruction	3
12 Testing	1
Total:	13 hours

This programme will be dealt with in more detail later, but here I must stress that it and the times given for each subject are the bare minimum necessary for the above-average student, and therefore your instructor may well spend longer on

it to satisfy himself that you are fully trained. You will probably find that your parachute club operates in co-operation with a flying club and so it is important that you know how to behave on an airfield. Each club has its own set of rules and no doubt your instructor will brief you about them. However, the following apply on any airfield:

1 Never smoke in hangars or in the close proximity of aircraft. The combination of aircraft dope and aviation fuel is a very real fire risk.

2 Be careful when handling light aircraft. They are normally covered in thin alloy and damage is very easily done. Any pilot will gladly show you where it is safe to push an aircraft or which parts you may use as a step to get in.

3 If an aircraft has its engine running, or is taxying, always stand

where the pilot can see you; remember, his visibility is probably more restricted than in the average car.

4 You should ways know which is the duty runway and normally this will be the runway running roughly in the same direction as the wind. Remember, light aircraft always land and take off into wind so if you do have to cross the duty runway, the most important way to look is downwind. On some airfields you will not be allowed to cross the duty runway but if you do, you should stop at least 20 yards short, kneel down (so that any pilot landing can clearly see your intention) and check carefully that there are no aircraft in the circuit. When all is clear you should move briskly across.

There may, of course, be other regulations which are particularly applicable to your own club and airfield. Make a note of them and make sure that you do everything you can to obey them. Sometimes these rules may seem unnecessary but in an aviation environment it is important that everybody obeys certain rules to ensure that everything is conducted safely.

Rules

There are certain rules that are common to all parachuting operations. First of all you may eventually become familiar with the BPA Operations Manual (available from the BPA Office; see page 9 for address). (Occasionally there is a need for the requirements of this manual to be amended as a result of new techniques and, when necessary, amendments will be produced by the Safety and Training Committee of the British Parachute Association.) Initially, however, you should know that sport parachuting within BPA affiliated clubs and centres should be conducted under the following ten basic rules:

1 Under arrangements made by a BPA advanced instructor who has been nominated as the club chief instructor (CCI) and who is normally present when parachuting is in progress.
2 By parachutists who are in every respect fit, trained, dressed, equipped, and briefed to undertake the descent planned.
3 When an adequate ground control organisation is in operation.
4 With an approved pilot, and jumpmaster qualified to despatch the parachutists concerned.
5 With parachutes in good condition, safe in all respects, correctly packed, well fitted and inspected before emplaning.
6 From an authorised aircraft suitably equipped and prepared for parachuting.
7 When wind conditions are suitable. Limitations in weather conditions are basically as follows:
   (a) *Wind* As a student you will not parachute if the surface wind exceeds 10 mph (9 kts or 4.5 metres a second).
   (b) *Cloud* You will not parachute if the cloud base is less than 2,000 ft above ground level and you should not intentionally drop or be dropped through cloud. The whole of the ground between the drop zone and where you leave the aircraft must be clear of any cloud.
   (c) *Visibility* You are only permitted to parachute in VMC (visual meteorological conditions), i.e. a horizontal visibility of at least 5 nautical miles.
8 On to an approved DZ (drop zone). (Normally an airfield or an open area of at least 600 metres in diameter constitutes an unrestricted DZ.
9 With all documentation in order and up-to-date.
10 According to the conditions laid down in the *BPA Operations Manual*.

The third basic rule given above concerns ground control organisation and this is important and needs to be explained in more detail. Having completed your ground training and been cleared to make your first parachute descent, the steps are as follows:

1 Draw your parachute equipment from the club's kit store.
2 Have your instructor put your name down on an aircraft load and make sure you know which one it is.
3 Make sure that you have been thoroughly briefed and inspected for the jump that you are going to do.
4 Keep a progress of the aircraft lifts in front of you and make sure that you are ready to come forward when called.
5 Emplane when directed and carry out and enjoy your first parachute jump.
6 After landing return to the club area and make sure you receive a comprehensive de-briefing on what you have achieved.

5. Aeroplanes

A sport parachute descent might best be described as being the time between fitting your equipment and removing it having made your parachute descent. As much of this time is spent in an aircraft it is important that you know about parachuting aeroplanes and how to move in the somewhat restricted fuselages. It will, therefore, be helpful to examine the type of aircraft suitable for sport parachuting and then to take a look at a few specific types.

The ideal parachuting aeroplane should have a high rate of climb, low running and maintenance costs, the ability to fly stably at less than 80 kts, a door which can be removed (or opened) in flight and which allows a clear exit, and finally it must be approved for parachuting by the Airworthiness Division of the Civil Aviation Authority.

The mainstay of smaller club aircraft are the various single-engined Cessnas—the Cessna 172 (can take 3 parachutists), the Cessna 180/182 (4 parachutists), the Cessna 185/206 (5 parachutists) and possibly the Cessna 207 (6 parachutists). They are all high-wing monoplanes which afford a simple exit from the step over the starboard wheel, or from the sill of a large door in the case of the Cessna 206 and 207. All the seats are removed from the fuselage except, of course, the pilot's. The

parachutist in charge of the load is called the 'jumpmaster' and he will be positioned kneeling facing forwards by the door, with the remaining parachutists on the load sitting two abreast on the floor facing the rear. There will be little room for movement and this can cause hazards which will be discussed later. Communication between parachutists and pilot can be verbal, visual by signalling with one hand in the pilot's mirror, or by using lights on the pilot's instrument panel controlled by a little switch above the door.

Another modern aircraft you might well use is the Cherokee 6 series. This is a low-wing monoplane which can carry the pilot and 6 parachutists in relative comfort. The parachutists are positioned in the aircraft as in the Cessna, facing the rear, with the jumpmaster sitting by the door facing forwards. The only disadvantage of this aircraft is the slightly smaller cabin compared with that of the Cessna, which makes movement even more difficult.

Many of the larger full-time parachute centres use the well-known Britten-Norman Islander aircraft, which is a twin-engined high-winged monoplane that can carry 8 parachutists sitting on the floor in much the same configuration as in the Cessna.

Movement in the Islander is relatively easy and the exit is made from a large door on the port side. Alternatively you may find yourself jumping from the high-winged single-engined 8 place Pilatus PC6 Turbo Porter. This remarkable aircraft has a similar cabin size to that of the Islander but its fast rate of climb ensures that you will not be sitting in it for very long! In many cases nowadays you may be lucky enough to find yourself jumping from an aircraft which has some form of in-flight door, which means that in winter months it will be much warmer inside and the aircraft door will only be opened just before exit.

In all cases until you have progressed to category 6 your jumpmaster will always be an instructor. The jumpmaster is responsible for the briefing of the pilot, for taking charge of the remaining parachutists, for lining up the aircraft (called 'spotting') and despatching all the parachutists safely over the correct point on the ground.

A word on parachuting (or 'jump') pilots at this stage is appropriate. Good parachuting pilots are few and far between for a variety of different reasons. Flying for parachuting has to be precise and requires a number of techniques that are not normally employed in other types of flying. The pilot must fly up to jump height

The Pilatus PC6 Turbo Porter on take off
with 8 parachutists on board.

as fast as he can and once he has dropped his jumpers, he must put the aircraft back down on the ground again as quickly as possible without over-cooling the engines. Once he is running the aircraft in over the drop zone he must use precise rudder turns. Normally a pilot turns an aircraft using aileron (or banked) turns which is more stable, but when spotting the jumpmaster has to be able to look straight down. Combine this with the fact that he is flying a heavily laden aircraft at take off, doing it many times during the day for long hours, and you will see that a parachuting pilot requires a singular kind of involvement in the sport. Don't, therefore, take him for granted.

The preparation of an aircraft for parachuting is normally fairly simple and should be carried out with your pilot's help or advice. It usually consists of removing the seats, securing seat-belts, removing any unnecessary equipment and taping up any sharp objects, especially near or around the door. The actual documentation involved will be undertaken by your club. However, it is worth knowing that all aircraft must have a current Certificate of Airworthiness which, when used for parachuting, must have those conditions spelt out. Also it will require a current Certificate of Maintenance.

Drills

There are routine 'drills' used in the aircraft, as well as drills for cases of emergency. Although the pilot of any aircraft is always in command of it and its passengers, and is

Pre-emplaning checks.

responsible for them, the jumpmaster must accept direct responsibility for the conduct of the jumpers. This sounds contradictory, but I hope by the end of the chapter you will see that it is not so, and that the pilot and jumpmaster in fact work as a team with the former

being the ultimate boss.

Aircraft drills will be covered very thoroughly by your instructor on the ground during your training, either by using a mock-up of the aircraft or the aircraft itself. The majority of parachuting aircraft have only just enough room for people to move around within their cabins and, therefore, from the beginning you should be constantly aware of the possibilities of catching pieces of your equipment either on other parachutists' equipment or on protrusions in the aircraft. The most dangerous of these possibilities is that of catching the reserve ripcord handle, thus releasing the pins and having the reserve canopy deploying within the aircraft. If this should happen and you spot it just as the canopy starts to appear, grab the whole reserve pack with both arms and clutch it to you firmly. If you are close to the open door, try to move away or turn your back towards it to prevent the slipstream tearing the canopy from your grip. If you are close to the door and the slipstream does catch hold of your reserve canopy and starts to deploy it within the aircraft, you really have got a problem. If you just sit tight the inflation of the canopy in the slipstream will either pull in a straight line, probably through the side of the fuselage, or will wrap itself around the tailplane with you on the end—it could even rip the tail fin or an elevator clean away, thus bringing the whole aircraft down. This all sounds very alarming but there is no problem so long as you react quickly and correctly. If you see the canopy start to snake out of the door, you must dive out after it and the chances are

that the jumpmaster will be assisting you by pushing you from behind. If this should happen all you can now do is enjoy the ride back to earth under the slightly smaller reserve canopy.

This drill should not be necessary if you protect your reserve handle with one hand and move carefully in the aircraft when you have to. If you feel any part of your equipment catch on something, do not pull against it—just relax, find the cause, sort it out and start again. Or, alternatively, inform the jumpmaster. It will be to your advantage and safer in the long run.

Now the aeroplane is ready for take off and this is something over which you have no control. The take off is critical because, particularly if the aircraft has just refuelled, it will be close to its all-up weight. Ensure that you keep still during take off and be mentally prepared for any aircraft emergency that might occur. If there is an engine failure during the latter half of the take-off run or soon after the aircraft has become airborne, there is little you can do apart from bracing yourself for the almost inevitable hard landing. If this should happen, once the aircraft has come to rest be prepared to evacuate it quickly and without panic. It may be that the landing has damaged the fuel system and a fire could result.

Once the aircraft has reached safe emergency jumping altitude, which can for general purposes be considered to be about 500 ft, you can relax to a certain extent, although here again an engine failure may necessitate abandoning the aircraft—this time by parachute. The obvious consideration here is the experience of the jumpers in the aircraft. The most inexperienced jumper is, naturally, the static line student. Normally all static lines will be hooked up to the strong-point and checked before take off. This means that if you have to leave the aircraft in flight in an emergency you will be using your main parachute. Obviously, in the unlikely event of this happening, the jumpmaster will decide whether the aircraft has reached sufficient altitude for a safe parachute descent to be made. Therefore, below 500 ft sit tight and brace yourself for the aircraft crashing; above 500 ft follow your jumpmaster's instructions and exit the aircraft as quickly as possible allowing the static line operated main parachute to bring you safely to the ground. In talking about these emergencies you can now see the importance of wearing your helmet during take off. The lessons here are obvious:

(a) learn all aircraft emergencies as a drill;

Always approach the aircraft from behind the wing.

(b) if an emergency occurs, keep calm, follow your jumpmaster's instructions; and

(c) carry out the drills as practised.

Normally instructions in the aircraft are given visually to avoid any confusion and all movements in the aircraft will be practised comprehensively on the ground. Because of the number of different aircraft in use it is simply not possible to detail all the moves for each aircraft type. Your instructor will go through them with you very thoroughly, showing you the exact positions of your hands and feet at any given moment. These drills will be practised until they become automatic, so that before your first descent your movements within the fuselage of the aircraft are lively and precise. Having reached the door, you will then have the problem of the exit itself, which is the next subject to tackle.

6. The stable position and the exit

The stable position

Mastering the 'stable' position is the key to your sport parachuting progress. When the parachute deploys, activated by either static line or ripcord when you have

Nick Cullum demonstrates a basic spread stable position.

progressed to freefall, it is essential that the parachutist is in such a position that the parachute is free to develop directly away from the body. With the main parachute mounted on his back, this body position must be such that the

parachutist has his back uppermost and his stomach towards the earth. If this position were reversed the parachutist would be turned around violently upon a canopy deployment, with the danger of parts of the parachute being

entangled with his extended limbs.

Initially you will be shown the basic (full spread) stable position. You will see that the basis is a well arched back combined with extended arms and legs. The head is forced back, with the back of the helmet against the top of the back-pack and the eyes on the horizon. The arms are spread out to each side of the body and are in line with the shoulders, while the legs are at an angle of about 45°, level with each other and slightly bent at the knees. If the arms are positioned too far forwards it will cause the head to rise up and a twisting of the body in freefall through a longitudinal axis, while if the arms are allowed to come too far back, the head will tend to drop. Any bending of the arms or legs asymmetrically may cause the body to turn around a vertical axis, or at worst may produce un-controlled tumbling.

Why does this position make you fall stomach-downwards and allow the parachute to deploy directly away from your body? The easiest way to illustrate it is to cut out of a piece of card the approximate silhouette of a parachutist in the full spread position, and then to bend it to the position of the basic stable spread. If you now hold your model skydiver against the ceiling the right way up and drop him, he will freefall to the floor remaining the right way up. If you repeat the operation, this

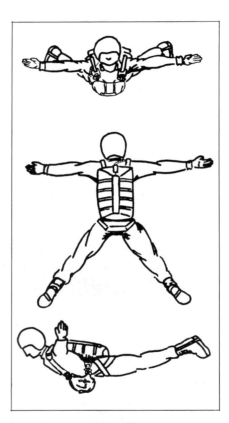

The full spread stable position.

time dropping him upside down, you will see him turn over and land the right way up. This basic spread position will be practised incessantly during your training until it becomes second nature and your stomach muscles feel extremely tired.

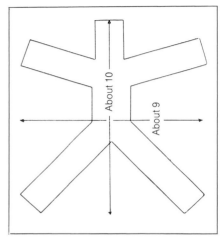

Template for card cut-out model of the stable position.

The exit

It can now be seen that the exit should be designed to enable you to attain the stable position as quickly and simply as possible. Basically there are two types of exit, dependent on the aircraft type in use.

The first type of exit is that which is used from the step located above the wheel, normally from the tricycle undercarriaged Cessnas. In this case you will be standing with your left foot on the step, holding with both hands to the wing strut and with your right foot trailing. The move to this position will be

It is important that you react to the exit command of 'GO!' on your first descent without hesitation. Therefore, this command will be used throughout your training for practising both exits and landing. You must get used to reacting immediately to this command: when you hear it for real you will have enough anxiety without thinking whether you should go or not. You should simply react as you have practised all through your ground training, without giving it a second thought.

The verbal count

This is very important and it gives a direct lead into the subject of parachuting emergency procedures. The verbal count is a vital aid to being aware of the number of seconds your parachute is taking to deploy. A second is very accurately accounted for by saying verbally 'One thousand' at your normal speaking rate. For the static line descent the verbal count is four seconds. So, on the word of command 'GO!' you launch yourself into the stable position and immediately start the verbal count by *shouting out loud* (loud enough for the pilot to hear!) 'One thousand, two thousand, three thousand, four thousand, check'. On the word 'check' look sharply over your shoulder and check that

practised again using the aircraft mock-up on the ground. Once you have reached this position, look in at your instructor signifying that you are ready to go and he will then tap you on the leg and shout the command 'GO!'

The second type of exit is that from the sitting position in the sill of the door. In this case you have to slide across the floor to a position where you are sitting with your feet out of the door of the aircraft facing forwards. This move and the final exit position will also be practised on the ground. Again, once your instructor is satisfied that you are ready to go, he will tap you on the shoulder and shout the exit command 'GO!'

Whichever exit is employed it is worth mentioning that you will be moving from the relative calm of the inside of the cabin of the aircraft to the slipstream outside the aircraft, which will be travelling at about 70 mph when you exit. Do not let this worry you but concentrate on pushing off firmly and forcing your body into the practised stable position when you are given the exit command 'GO!'

Jackie Smith demonstrates a beautiful dive exit from a Stampe flown by the author.

the canopy is deploying satisfactorily. Whatever the count (it may vary slightly from club to club), the instructor will go through it very thoroughly. The verbal count, however, is something you can practise yourself in conjunction with the exercises described earlier; so when you give yourself the command of 'GO!' shout out the count, at the same time going through the motions described. Hold the necessary position until you have finished the count . . . then relax. Make sure you actually shout out the count, because this is what you will be doing when you do it for real and if you get into the habit of just saying it to yourself, then you will surely forget to count at all when you actually carry out a live descent.

A handstand exit off the tailgate of a large helicopter is not for students!

7. Emergencies

The key word in the conduct of the sport of parachuting is *safety* and so your ability to deal with any out-of-the-ordinary situation is of paramount importance. This section deals with parachute malfunctions and the procedures (to be carried out as drills) to be employed in each case to give you a safe landing. Do not take the likelihood of your encountering a parachute malfunction out of context—it will very rarely occur but it would be irresponsible not to train very carefully for every eventuality and learn how to cope with it.

Parachute malfunctions are normally caused by one (or a combination) of the following: faulty equipment, bad parachute packing, or a poor body position during canopy deployment. Faulty equipment is less and less liable to contribute to a parachute malfunction as the standard of parachute equipment is improving all the time and very strict controls are exercised in the case of new equipment coming onto the market. Gone are the pioneer days when jumpers were equipped with parachutes of extremely doubtful origins and varying states of airworthiness. Initially you are likely to use well-maintained club equipment and a point worth

making at this stage is that if you decide to buy your own, make sure your chief instructor or qualified rigger checks it out thoroughly before you part with the cash.

Bad parachute packing is unlikely to cause a malfunction during your student days for two reasons: firstly, when you initially start packing your own parachute it is quite extraordinary how meticulous you will be; and, secondly, until you are granted a packing certificate, an instructor or qualified parachute packer will carefully check each stage of your packing. However, once you are qualified to pack your own

parachute there is a tendency to become lax and you must not fall into the trap of taking parachute packing for granted. Experience has shown that poor or sloppy parachute packing is the prime cause of canopy malfunctions. A poor body position during canopy deployment is another likely cause of a malfunction during your early descents, and that is why the previous chapter is so important.

Your biggest enemy in the unlikely event of you having a malfunction is *Time*. Experience and the possibility of a malfunction have produced an opening height for the main parachute of 2,000 ft above

He only has 2 or 3 seconds to react to this situation.

ground level. Therefore, with no parachute and falling at terminal velocity of 120 mph (176 ft per second) it would take you between 12 and 14 seconds to reach the ground. This means that, in the worst case of a total malfunction (complete non-appearance of the parachute) and allowing for your reaction time, carrying out the drill as taught and your reserve parachute deploying, you should be safely suspended under your reserve well above 1,000 ft AGL. Any partial malfunction (i.e. part of the canopy deployed) will slow your rate of descent and thus give you more time to sort out the problem.

Once you have exited the aircraft (on a static line descent) and have reached the end of the verbal count at the word 'check', look sharply over your shoulder to make sure that your parachute is deploying correctly. If your verbal count has not been garbled (the most usual tendency) and has taken the correct time, you will find that by the time you have shouted 'check' you will already have been pulled into a vertical position by the deploying parachute which will be billowing out above you. All you have to do is watch the canopy fill out completely with air if it hasn't done so already. This, therefore, is the practice, assuming that the parachute deploys normally. If, however, when you shout 'check' you look over

your shoulder and see nothing, you may have encountered a malfunction.

This is the moment to describe the standard reserve deployment drill, which you will practise constantly during your training until it becomes second nature. *Look for the reserve handle—grasp firmly with the right hand—place the left hand round the front of the reserve container—feet together—pull the handle and throw it away—grab the reserve canopy with both hands and throw it hard, down and away from you.* This procedure is standard for all malfunctions in your student days but may be modified when you have gained more experience. It is important that you understand each possible type of malfunction.

Malfunctions

The first is the *pilot-chute hesitation* (or burble) and is caused by one of two things: either your body position on canopy deployment is such that it accentuates the low pressure area (or partial vacuum in the small of your back caused by your passage through the air), or the coiled spring in your pilot-chute may be too weak. In the first case it is possible that your pilot-chute leaves the pack tray but bobs around in the low pressure area and cannot be deployed by your body's slipstream.

Neither of these possibilities could occur on a static line descent but the eventuality could arise when you progress to freefall: therefore, you must know the cure. On the word 'check' you may or may not observe the pilot-chute bobbing around in the small of your back, but you should carry out the reserve procedure immediately. If this is done correctly it will have the effect of turning you over and allowing the direct air-flow past your body to catch the pilot-chute and thus deploy the main canopy in the normal way, possibly even before you have a chance to pull the reserve handle. But the drill during your first few descents must be to pull the reserve handle right away, although there will be the possibility of the main and reserve deploying together. After a few descents it will be expected that you either pause for a second with your right hand on the reserve handle, to see if the main does deploy as explained above, or you eliminate the low pressure area by dipping one shoulder and thus allowing the slipstream to grab the pilot-chute.

The next possible malfunction is the least likely: it is the *total malfunction*. In this case the count has been completed and nothing at all has appeared. It could be caused (on static line) by a failure of the static line, but this is highly unlikely. On freefall it could be

The student reserve assembly with centre pull handle and FXC 12000 A.O.D.

caused by some form of pack closure where the sides of the container do not open, but whatever reason you can analyse the cause on the ground. Of possible malfunctions this one is the easiest with which to deal because there is no partly deployed canopy to interfere with the deployment of the reserve. Don't delay—pull your reserve handle right away. The important thing to remember while you practise this drill is that, although it is the easiest malfunction to rectify, you will have the least time in which to carry it out. During your first few descents you will not be able to differentiate between the pilot-chute hesitation and the total malfunction; this should not worry you, just react immediately and deploy the reserve.

The *'streamer' malfunction* is an unusual one whereby the rigging lines deploy, pulling you into an upright position, but the canopy does not inflate—there could be one or two reasons for this but in the middle of a descent is not the time to find out why! The resultant drag will decrease your rate of descent very slightly but here again you must react quickly. Do not try to shake the main open but go straight for the reserve handle. As you pull the handle keep both hands spread in front of you to prevent the reserve deploying straight up into the main.

The next consideration is the *partial malfunction*, which can vary from being stable to spinning violently, or from a division of the canopy into two brassiere-shaped lobes (the 'Mae West') to a canopy which is badly torn. Basically there are two methods of deploying the

The 'streamer' malfunction.

Reserve deployment drill.

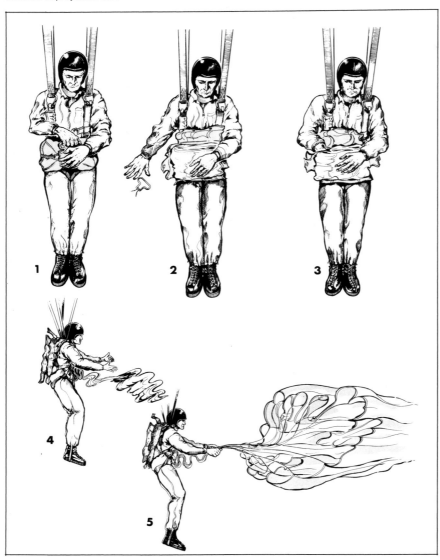

1
2
3
4
5

reserve parachute should you experience a partial malfunction. The first is to deploy the reserve with the partial malfunction still above you. The second is to cut away the main parachute before deploying the reserve parachute. Until you have gained further qualifications, the first system is that which you will use and it should be practised until it becomes automatic. The second system, of the cut-away, is the safer, however, when you start to jump with high performance canopies.

Twists

Twists in the rigging lines can easily occur during canopy deployment. In themselves they need not be considered as a malfunction but two vital points must be made. If on checking the canopy you cannot look up, it may be that long twists in the lines are preventing you from raising your head to carry out the check. In this case you must assume the worst as you can't check the main, so initiate the reserve deployment sequence right away. Secondly, if when you carry out the canopy check you see you have twists in the lines, make sure you look above them and concentrate on examining the canopy first. If the latter gives cause for alarm do not hesitate and operate your reserve parachute immediately. On the other hand, if the main canopy is all right, you can

The ripcord pull and deployment...
with concurrent emergency count.

kick out of the twists, at the same time pulling the risers apart, before starting to steer the canopy in the normal way.

A pilot-chute on the reserve parachute will obviously cause a canopy to deploy more quickly, especially in the case of a total malfunction or cut-away; but the disadvantage of this system is that if a pilot-chuted reserve is deployed under a rotating or spinning malfunction, there is a very real danger of losing control and having it 'barber-pole' around the partial malfunction. The advantage of not having a pilot-chute in the reserve parachute is that you will have more control of the reserve canopy should you be forced to deploy it while you still have a partial malfunction flying above you. Therefore, until you are jumping a sophisticated sport parachute you will not be equipped with a pilot-chute on the reserve and should not cut-away in the event of a partial malfunction. However, once you are further qualified and when you start jumping high performance sport parachutes, you should never deploy a reserve under a partial malfunction, as it will almost certainly be rotating. In this case you must cut away immediately and deploy the pilot-chuted reserve parachute. The deployment of the reserve parachute, which is not equipped with a pilot-chute, is

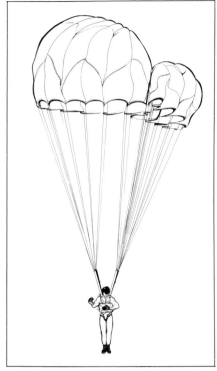

The 'Mae West' malfunction.

Partial malfunctions

The simplest partial malfunctions you may encounter are those of the stable variety which could be broken lines, a torn canopy or the stable Mae West, or any combination of the three. There is, of course, no cure for the first two, but the third is slightly different. The Mae West malfunction is easily recognised as the canopy divides into two or more lobes on deployment, caused by the rigging lines catching over the top of the canopy or by the lower peripheral hem blowing back over the canopy to produce a similar condition. If your rate of descent is not too great—other jumpers in the sky will give you a guide—you may spend a *short* time trying to clear the Mae West (sometimes called the 'thrown line' or 'blown periphery', BP), by pulling down sharply on the lines which appear to be causing it. If this treatment does not clear the malfunction immediately then you must deal with it as previously taught. The reserve should now obviously inflate, but if the main is giving you plenty of support it may well just collapse down by your legs; don't worry—this is a sign that the malfunction is not a severe one and you will have time to pull the reserve canopy in and attempt to fly it again. If the malfunction is serious, the reserve canopy will virtually deploy on its own, but you should

be careful it does not tangle with the main as it inflates. Once the two canopies are flying it is a good idea to rest your forearms on the reserve rigging lines to try to keep it clear of the main. The seriously malfunctioned main will probably collapse completely after full deployment of the reserve and in this case it is a good idea to jettison the remnants of the main using the canopy releases, or to haul it in and hold the bundle between your legs to get it out of the way until you land.

As you become more experienced a slight variation may be added: as the canopy starts to appear from the pack hold it firmly with the left hand and slide the right hand under the canopy and grasp the lower peripheral hem. Now throw it outwards as described above and in doing so grab the lower peripheral hem with the left hand, about 2 ft from the right hand. By shaking the canopy like a blanket with both hands the deployment is speeded up, but when using this refinement it is important that the reserve is packed with the peripheral hem on the right-hand side.

A partial malfunction which is asymmetric in nature will almost certainly rotate, and this rotation can build up at an alarming rate. This particular malfunction, therefore, needs to be dealt with swiftly for two reasons:

nowadays often assisted by an enclosed spring which is positioned between the folded canopy and the stowed suspension lines. On deployment this enclosed spring (or 'zebedee') will push the canopy away from the pack tray and fall to the ground, and will not in any way hinder the deployment of the reserve.

(a) the rotation will almost certainly get faster, and

(b) the longer you wait before taking any emergency action, the more likelihood there is of you becoming disorientated. So quickly take the decision to deploy your reserve and carry out the procedure already described.

Once you have qualified as a Category 8 parachutist (according to the BPA system) you will almost certainly be using a high performance canopy. You will also have a pilot-chute attached to the apex of the reserve parachute. A main parachute harness will be equipped with some form of canopy release; most common are the traditional 'Capewell' canopy releases and the more modern 'Three Ring Circus' type. You must be thoroughly familiar with whatever canopy release system is used on your main harness and with its operation. The problem of deploying the reserve parachute while still attached to a partially malfunctioned main parachute is the danger of entanglement between the two. Once you have more experience this situation will be avoided by your being able to initiate a cut-away of the main parachute before deployment of the reserve. Once again the cut-away procedure should be initiated swiftly as a malfunctioned high

performance canopy will almost certainly rotate much more quickly than a malfunctioned student parachute.

The cut-away procedure

The cut-away procedure is straightforward. On checking the canopy and discovering the malfunction it is acceptable to spend a couple of seconds trying to clear it providing you are still above 2,000 ft. Once you have passed through 2,000 ft you are committed to cutting away in order to have the reserve flying by 1700 ft AGL at the lowest. Having made the decision *do not hesitate*. First, get rid of the main ripcord handle (if you don't the loose end could become entangled with the deploying reserve). Secondly, ensure a back-to-earth position when you cut away—round your back and shoulders, and spread your legs in front of you. Thirdly, check the position of the reserve handle. Fourthly, check there is no one immediately below you and then, finally and swiftly yet precisely, initiate the canopy release and *immediately you are free of the main parachute pull the reserve handle – do not try to get stable*. If you are using a tandem system with the reserve mounted above the main there is no need to adopt a back-to-earth position before you cut away. It is important that this procedure is

practised regularly and preferably in a suspended harness.

Tears in canopies and/or the odd broken line do not necessarily require use of the reserve parachute, but remember that the decision to use the reserve is entirely yours and if there is any doubt at all then it is safer to rely on the reserve parachute. Never allow yourself to become complacent about the reserve parachute or its use, and make sure that it is re-packed at intervals of 90 days at least. You never know when you may need it. There are a number of reserve canopies on the market and depending on your weight it is worth seeking an instructor's advice as to which kind is best suited to you individually. Most reserve parachutes are now steerable and this, of course, is almost essential when parachuting on to more restricted drop zones, e.g. displays. Again, whatever type of canopy you use make sure you are thoroughly familiar with it and its potential performance.

The hang-up

There is a special procedure for coping with an emergency of a slightly different nature called the 'hang-up'. The hang-up is when a static line student exits the aircraft and becomes suspended beneath it either by his static line or a fouled canopy. It is exceptionally rare and if it does occur it will probably have been caused by a poor body position on exit and the static line not being properly controlled by the instructor; or a premature deployment of the canopy for some other reason. Whatever the cause the outcome of the student dangling beneath the aircraft is a very tricky state of affairs and, of course, the smaller the aircraft, the more difficult it will be for the pilot to remain in control. However, the procedure is very straightforward. If you are conscious, in control of your faculties and fully understand the drill, you signal this to your instructor by placing both hands on your helmet. Your instructor will then show you a knife which indicates that he is going to cut you free. He will not do this, however, until you have placed your hand over the reserve ripcord handle. (Do not grasp the handle at this stage in case you initiate a premature deployment of the reserve parachute while you are still caught.) Do not pull the reserve handle until your instructor has cut through the static line (or fouled canopy) because of the danger of the reserve deploying while you are still attached—if this happens it will give the pilot very severe problems indeed! So, the instant you are cut free, pull the reserve handle violently and throw it away. Now, hopefully, you can relax and enjoy the safe

ride back to earth. If you are not in control of your faculties, all you need to know at this stage is that your instructor will climb down the static line and cut you free deploying the reserve parachute for you. He will then fall free and deploy his own main parachute. The hang-up drill is unlikely to be required as the situation arises very infrequently; but having said that, as with all emergencies, it is important that you fully understand and practise the drills.

Automatic opening devices
You may well find that the club at which you start to parachute is equipped with automatic opening devices for the reserve parachute. There are a number of different kinds available but whatever kind is in use will be explained to you in some detail by your instructor. In simple terms the barometrically operated AOD will function when you pass through a pre-determined height at a faster than acceptable rate of descent. The only thing that you need be aware of is the simple step of switching it off once the main canopy has successfully deployed. All automatic opening devices make the almost infallible student parachuting systems safer still and are an important contribution to your safety in the sport.

There is just a small chance that an accidental deployment of the

reserve parachute may occur either during or after the successful deployment of the main parachute. If the main and reserve deploy simultaneously there is a possibility of the two entangling, but there is little you can do at this stage to prevent it happening. If you do find yourself in the situation of two canopies deployed above you there is then little likelihood of entanglement, but the alternative is to continue the descent having hauled down the reserve and having tucked it away between your legs. If you find this too difficult to do simply rest your hands on the lines of the reserve parachute in an effort to keep it away from the main. Your rate of descent will be very little different from that under a fully deployed main parachute as the two canopies will fly at an angle to one another. All you can do is to hang there and take whatever landing is available to you in the normal way.

Finally, and with no apologies for repeating myself, remember that although you may never need to use the reserve parachute only correct teaching and constant practice will ensure that, should the necessity arise, you will carry out the emergency procedures with confidence and skill. Only when you can guarantee this can you consider yourself to be a safety-conscious sport parachutist.

8. Canopy control

The actual parachute descent under a fully deployed canopy can be divided into three distinct phases. First is the checking of the canopy and orientation; second is the steering of the canopy to land you in the target area; and third is the preparation for the landing itself. Before examining these parts of the descent in detail it is necessary to look at the factors that affect both your vertical rate of descent and horizontal speed across the ground.

The first factor is, of course, your own weight; the heavier you are, the faster you are likely to descend. Your weight has a direct influence on the next factor, which is the overall performance of your parachute canopy—its rate of descent and inherent forward speed. Generally speaking, these two factors remain constant but the other factors are variables that are governed by the natural elements in which we live. The higher the drop zone is above sea level, the greater the rate of descent due to the thinning of the atmosphere; actually this rate of descent increase is relatively insignificant and will not affect you as much as the type of ground over which you pass during your descent. The reason for this is that certain types of ground absorb heat quicker than others, and the resultant warmth will decrease your rate of descent as you pass through

it. Woods and ploughed fields are examples, but the one you are most likely to encounter is tarmac or concrete when you pass over runways on airfields. On a warm summer day it is not uncommon to feel your rate of descent decreased to practically nothing when passing over a warm runway. The most relevant variable, however, is the wind.

Wind

When considering the effect of wind it is necessary to understand both its speed and direction. Wind speed is normally measured in miles an hour, but may also be measured in knots (nautical miles per hour) or metres per second. The following table gives the comparisons:

wind speed conversion table

metres/ second	mph
1	2·25
2	4·5
3	6·75
4	9
5	11·25
6	13·5
7	15·75
8	18

The only method of measuring wind speed accurately is by the use of a calibrated anemometer. Ignore other indications such as wind-

socks or flags as these essentially are only a guide to wind direction. (Other means of determining wind direction are, of course, smoke, washing on lines, and the movement of clouds or foliage.) Initially you will only be concerned with how the wind speed and direction affect you once your canopy has deployed but, of course, later it is important to understand how it can affect you during the freefall phase of the descent.

To ensure that you land in the right area of the airfield it is important that your instructor despatches you over the correct point on the ground. This technique is called 'spotting' and the skill is explained later (see page 83). Suffice to say at this stage that your drift under the canopy is measured using a wind drift indicator (WDI). It is a strip of brightly coloured crepe paper, 20 ft long and 10 in wide, with a weighted rod taped to one end. When rolled up it should weigh about 3 oz; this will cause it to descend, having unrolled after being thrown from the aircraft, at a speed which is very similar to that of the average parachutist's rate of descent under an inflated canopy. A WDI, therefore, gives the instructor a very accurate idea of the wind speed and direction. It will enable him to decide over which point on the ground he will despatch you from the aeroplane (the WDI is normally dropped at the beginning of any parachuting session).

During your briefing your instructor will explain a point on the ground over which you will be despatched. This pre-determined point is called the 'opening point' (OP). Assuming you have been despatched in the area of the opening point you will then have a very fair chance of arriving safely in the target area, assuming you have handled your parachute canopy correctly.

Whatever the wind speed over the DZ, the target area can be reached by using good canopy control.

Air pressure

Air pressure which is inherent within all student parachute canopies can be directed through steering windows located in the rear of the canopy. The air pressure escaping through these steering windows will give the canopy an inherent forward speed. It may be easiest to visualise this escaping air pressure as a simple jet which propels the canopy forwards. The average student canopy has an inherent forward speed of somewhere in the region of 5–7 mph and a vertical rate of descent between 16 and 18 ft per second. Therefore, from an average canopy opening height of 2,500 ft AGL it will take the average parachutist about 2½ minutes to reach the ground. In a theoretical still air situation the canopy will simply move forwards across the ground in whichever direction it is pointed at its inherent forward speed of 5–7 mph; if the canopy remains facing in the same direction for the 2½ minutes of the descent it will cover about 365 yards.

The problem is that you will almost certainly never parachute in total still air conditions; there will

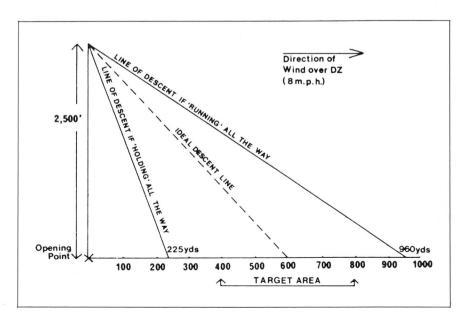

almost certainly be some sort of wind about. This inevitably makes canopy control a little more complicated than just a theoretical exercise. Supposing a canopy has an inherent forward speed of 5 mph and there is a wind speed over the DZ of 8 mph. If the canopy is faced downwind for the entire descent it will cover some 960 yards. However, if it is faced into wind for the entire descent it will only move about 225 yards from the opening point. If the canopy is moving downwind this is called 'running', while if the canopy is faced into wind it is called 'holding'. You can see, therefore, that even in fairly gentle conditions it is possible to have a variation of over 700 yards in your landing area. You will, however, be despatched over a pre-determined opening point which will allow you the best chance of landing midway between these two extremes. It is worth noting at this stage that for your first 20 or so descents it is only necessary for you to land within the *approximate* area of the target; so in referring to the target area initially, think of it as any grass area within about a 200-yard radius of the target cross.

Control of the parachute

Understanding how the canopy is controlled is simplicity itself. On the back of each of the two rear risers you will find the steering toggles, one on each side. Each steering line runs up through a keeper and is attached to the rigging line, which goes up to the outside of each steering window. If the left-hand steering line is pulled down this distorts and reduces the effective area of the left-hand steering window. The result of this is that relatively more air pressure is permitted to escape through the right-hand steering window; therefore, the canopy will turn around to the left. Likewise, if the right-hand toggle is pulled down, the right-hand steering window is reduced in size, relatively more air is forced from the left-hand window and the canopy will turn around to the right.

This theory can be applied to the three stages of the descent. Returning to the stage of the 'check', that is exactly what you must do. First grasp the risers and look up so that you can see the entire canopy. Check the canopy for any of the abnormalities discussed in the emergency section and do not mistake the steering windows for anything out of the ordinary. Follow the check of the canopy by examining the rigging and steering lines down to the risers and steering toggles respectively. If all is well, grasp the steering toggles with the second and third fingers of each hand and have a good look

around, above and below you. It is unlikely that there will be any other parachutists close to you as plenty of time will be given between inexperienced parachutists, but this quick look round is a good habit to acquire for later on.

Having carried out these checks, you should now see where you are in relation to the ground. The aircraft will have run in over the target into wind, and if you have exited correctly, i.e. facing forwards and over a pre-determined opening point upwind of the target, you can expect to be hanging under the canopy, over this opening point and with your back to the target. If your back is not towards the target it may well be that you have turned around the vertical axis before or during canopy deployment and in this eventuality it is best to turn so that the target is behind you; the purpose of this is to ensure that you are holding into wind while you are checking your relative position to the ground.

Now look straight down below and see if you are in fact over the opening point. If you are upwind of the opening point, or 'deep', you can expect to run a good deal during your descent towards the target and, conversely, if you are downwind or 'short' of your opening point, you can expect to hold for a large part of the descent. If, however, you are to the left or right

45

The canopy well under control, with the hands where they can be seen.

of your opening point, you are positioned 'off the wind line'. The wind line is an imaginary line running through the centre of the target in exactly the same direction as the wind; it follows, therefore, that the opening point is always on this imaginary line. The wind line is the crux to accurate parachuting, for if you stray too far away from it, it may well be difficult to manoeuvre yourself back to it before the descent is complete. There is,

however, an area of manoeuvre away from the wind line which will still permit you an accurate landing and this area is called the 'wind cone'. During your first few descents your main problem will be not knowing your exact height off the ground, or how long it is going to take you to descend the rest of the way. Experience is the only solution to the problem and to this end you should note the size of buildings, vehicles, trees and other familiar objects on the ground during the orientation phase of your descent.

The target area
Now you have established where you are it is possible to control your parachute towards the target area. The easiest way to learn canopy control is to have an instructor talk you down from the ground and this is most effectively done with ground-to-air radios, but visual systems are also in use at some clubs. You need not expect to be talked down on every descent, and sooner or later you can expect to fend for yourself. In any event after each of your early descents you will

Canopy control.

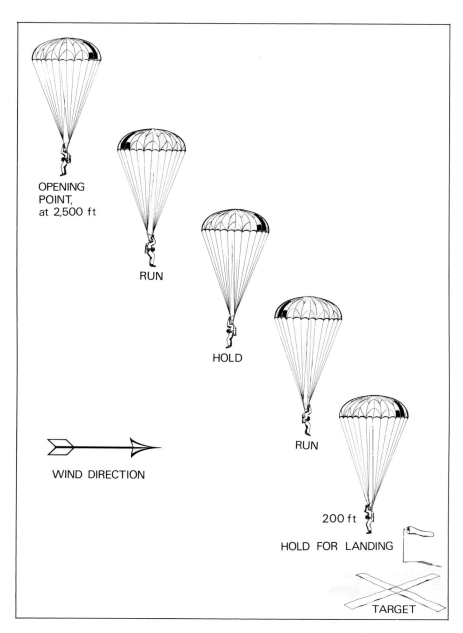

OPENING
POINT,
at 2,500 ft

RUN

HOLD

RUN

200 ft
HOLD FOR LANDING

TARGET

WIND DIRECTION

have a thorough debriefing on your canopy handling by your instructor who will inform you why you did or did not land in the target area.

From your first descent onwards get used to the habit of controlling your canopy with gentle but positive movements of your hands. Any violent tugging of the steering toggles will immediately upset the inherent stability and trim of the canopy in flight; additionally, alteration of canopy trim will increase the rate of descent. Therefore, do make sure that all movements are gentle ones. Having said that, however, it is obvious that the further down you pull the toggle on one particular side, the faster will be the turn in that direction. (Also the rate of descent will be proportionately increased.) It is useful to move your hands slightly in front of you so that you can see them and be aware of where they need to be positioned for any particular condition of flight. If both steering toggles are pulled down simultaneously, the inherent forward speed of the canopy is reduced or 'braked'. There is little purpose in trying to brake a round canopy's inherent forward speed, but this is something that you will be very aware of when progressing to the use of square parachutes.

The ideal approach to the target area is made by you keeping it in sight throughout the descent.

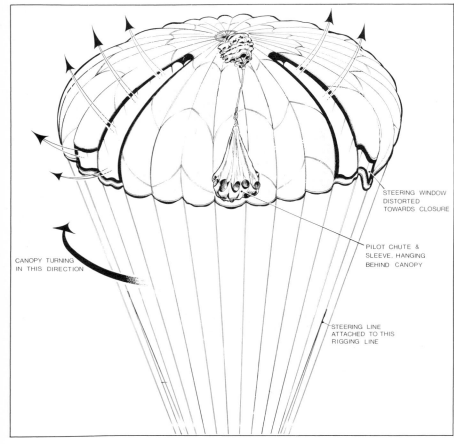

CANOPY TURNING
IN THIS DIRECTION

STEERING WINDOW
DISTORTED
TOWARDS CLOSURE

PILOT CHUTE &
SLEEVE. HANGING
BEHIND CANOPY

STEERING LINE
ATTACHED TO THIS
RIGGING LINE

A 'double L' canopy undergoing a right turn.

A 'GQ Aeroconical' facing into wind for landing.

Holding, therefore, is not very productive as your back is towards the target and you have to give small turns to left or right to keep a visual check on your relative position. Your limit of manoeuvre away from the wind line will be dependent on, firstly, the inherent performance of the parachute canopy and, secondly, the speed of the wind over the drop zone.

The ideal spot will permit you a gentle zigzag path to the target, manoeuvring astride the wind line. Of course, you must check your position in relation to the target at regular intervals during the descent; it may help you to bear in mind that after about 30 seconds of your descent you should be positioned about a quarter of the way from the opening point to the target, after 60

seconds halfway, after $1\frac{1}{2}$ minutes three quarters of the way, and very close to it after 2 minutes. If at any time you think you are going to undershoot, then you must make up more distance by running towards the target and, conversely, if you think you are going to overshoot you must hold into wind to slow your movement towards it. The tidiest way, however, is to alter the zigzag path to ensure that you are facing the target area for the majority of the descent. In any event, experience is the most effective school combined with comprehensive guidance from your instructor.

A. For a wind speed over the DZ of 10 mph.
B. For a wind speed of 5 mph.

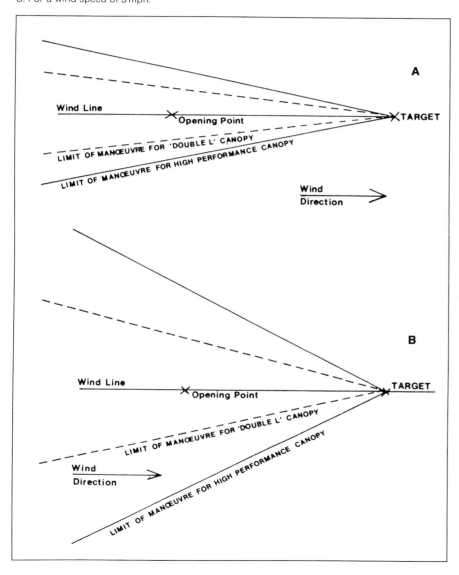

A

Wind Line
Opening Point
TARGET

LIMIT OF MANŒUVRE FOR 'DOUBLE L' CANOPY
LIMIT OF MANŒUVRE FOR HIGH PERFORMANCE CANOPY

Wind
Direction

B

Wind Line
Opening Point
TARGET

LIMIT OF MANŒUVRE FOR 'DOUBLE L' CANOPY
LIMIT OF MANŒUVRE FOR HIGH PERFORMANCE CANOPY

Wind
Direction

Landing

The final phase of the descent is the preparation for the landing. As with aeroplanes, all parachute landings are made facing into wind. The reason for this is that the effectiveness of the surface wind is reduced by the inherent forward speed of the canopy acting against it, thus reducing or even stopping your forward speed over the ground. (If this speed of the wind is more than the inherent forward speed of the canopy you can expect to be moving backwards for the descent, but this is not a problem, as will be seen later.) You must ensure the canopy is facing directly into wind for your landing and, secondly, you must avoid any substantial manipulation of the canopy within the last 250 ft (about 15 seconds) of the descent. Remember any manipulation of the canopy will upset its trim and rate of descent and of course this is not desirable just prior to the landing.

Before you emplane you will be briefed on the wind direction and which way to face for the landing by having easy references pointed out to you. However, do not forget to look at the wind sock as the wind may well change in direction. Once you are sure you are facing into wind you must now concentrate on adopting and holding the parachute landing position in final preparation for the actual moment

(a) When you find yourself positioned deep (up-wind) of the target on orientation.
(b) When you find yourself positioned short (down-wind) of the opening point on orientation.
(c) When you find yourself positioned over the opening point itself on orientation.

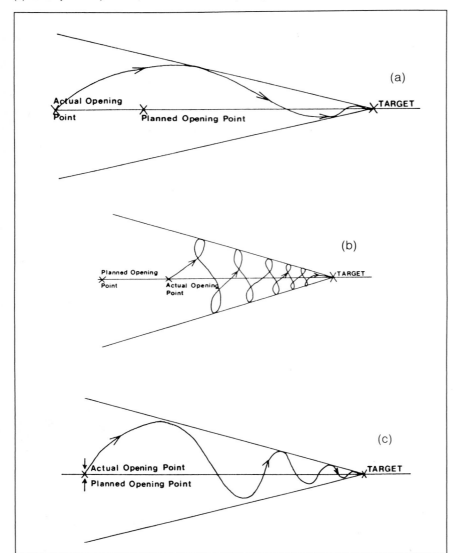

A ram-air canopy on deep brakes.

of touchdown. Until you are better experienced you can expect to be using a round parachute and the principles described will cover your early progression. Once you have qualified further, e.g. as a BPA Category 8 parachutist, you may then progress to using a square or 'Ram-Air' canopy.

9. Parachute landings

Injuries in sport parachuting are most likely to occur as a result of a poorly executed landing—this may have been aided and abetted by poor canopy handling or a malfunctioned parachute, but the practised ability to cope with all possible types of landing will do much to reduce the risk of a landing injury.

Obviously there are some parts of the human frame that are more capable of withstanding the impact of landing than others. Therefore, the effective and safe landing is one that utilises those parts of the body most suited to absorbing the landing shock. In this context the actual bodily parachute landing position is of vital importance and its adoption must become second nature.

Landing position

The parachute landing position must be examined in detail, starting with the feet because ideally they will come into contact with the ground first! If you step from a train or bus the natural instinct is to land on your toes: in parachuting this may be acceptable when you have gained considerable experience, but in the early days it is important that before landing the soles of your feet

Jackie Smith demonstrates a good parachute landing position on the fan trainer.

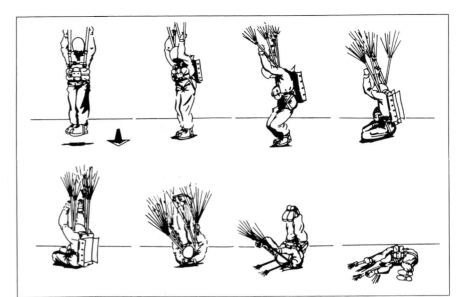

are positioned parallel to the ground, as the direction of landing is something over which you may not have total control. Your feet and knees should be forced tightly together, with the latter slightly bent so that you can just see your toes over your knees when hanging in the harness. This allows your lower limbs to be supple and relaxed but at the same time each leg is giving splint-like support to the other. Your back should be rounded with your chin locked down on to your chest, which eliminates possible injury during a backward landing since the head is prevented from being whipped back at the moment of impact. Finally, the arms are positioned upwards, with the elbows tucked in and to the front, and the hands grasping the steering toggles.

The good parachute landing position, therefore, achieves two vital aims. First, the impact of landing is absorbed by the most suitable parts of the body—soles of the feet, side of the leg, thighs, buttocks, and rounded back; and second, the vulnerable parts of the body, particularly the crotch and the face, are protected.

As you could be travelling in any direction across the ground just before touch down, it is important that you can take a landing in any direction. Landings can, therefore, be categorised as side landings (left

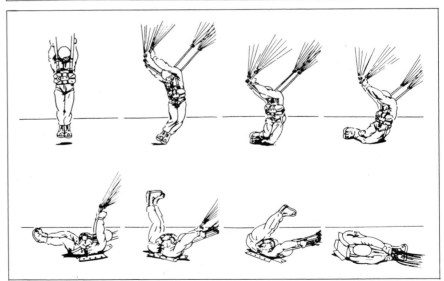

Forward left landing.

and right), forward landings (left and right) and backward landings (left and right). To understand each type of landing in detail you should study the diagrams. The simplest to master at first are the side landings, since just before touch down your feet are naturally at right-angles to

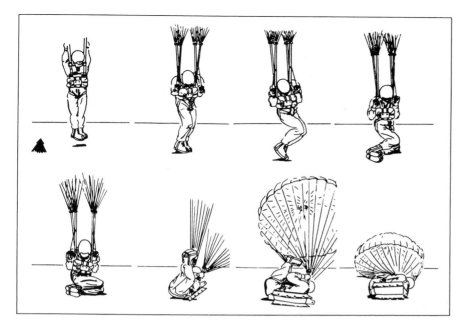

your line of drift (or movement across the ground). As you approach the ground sideways you should push your legs slightly into the line of drift to assist you in touching down on the soles of your feet together. As the feet touch, the upper part of the body is turned so that the roll finishes on the opposite shoulder. (If you are taking a side right landing, the right shoulder is turned forwards, and vice versa.)

For the forward landings your feet should be turned off to left or right as near to right-angles to the forward line of drift as possible. If your toes are pointing diagonally to the left, then a forward right landing will be taken, and vice versa. The forward landing is made with the upper part of the body turning so that you finish the roll on the opposite shoulder. The backward

landing is exactly opposite to the forward one, with the exception that your legs should be pushed back slightly from the hips to take the initial shock. Here again, the feet are turned off to be as near right-angled to the line of drift as possible, and the landing proceeds in the way already described.

Much of your training time will be spent on you learning and thoroughly practising parachute landings so that they become completely second nature. There are a number of different landing training aids, and you will progress from practising landings from a standing position, through jumping off a low ramp, to possibly a fan exit trainer which gives a realistic idea of the speed of landing. Some people take to landing or parachute landing falls (PLFs) more readily

than others and it is not unusual for instructors to single out those individuals who are not so supple or adept at landings to give them extra practice. Don't worry if this should happen in your case because it is important that your instructor is satisfied that you can absorb the shock of landing, by utilising a good PLF in any direction, before he allows you to make your parachute descent. Anything less than that and he will not have been responsible in his duties as an instructor.

The last point that must be made is that it is imperative you adopt and maintain the described parachute landing position before and during the touch down. The usual fault is to point your toes and to reach for the ground—you are going to land sooner or later anyway, so remember: arms up; elbows tucked in; head bent forwards; chin on chest; back rounded; watch the ground; feet and knees tight together, the former parallel to the ground and the latter slightly bent; and finally, be semi-relaxed. If you have achieved a good standard of PLFs during your training it will stand you in good stead later. Many landings will be extremely gentle, but once in a while, maybe under a reserve or malfunctioned main, you will have to absorb a fast landing. This is where good training will come into

its own and prevent you from receiving injury.

Canopy collapse

Having touched down safely, you must now collapse the canopy. In normal student wind conditions it is likely that the canopy will collapse on its own anyway, but it may be that a gust of wind will keep the canopy inflated. It is important that you stand up as soon as possible after the landing so that the drop zone controller can see you are unhurt; if you remain lying on the ground it is indicative to him that you may be injured and he will take action accordingly. The easiest way to collapse the canopy is to scramble to your feet as briskly as possible and then to run around the canopy turning it out of the wind. If a colleague has landed closely or there are people nearby, one of them could grab the apex and effectively do the same thing by pulling the canopy out of wind for you. The third method which you could use if the wind prevented you from jumping up and running round the canopy, is to pull in handfuls of rigging lines near the ground and keep pulling them in hand over hand until the canopy collapses from the ground upwards. (If you pull on the rigging lines that run to the top of the canopy as it is lying on the ground you will find it almost

Students returning from the drop zone.

impossible to collapse the canopy because you are pulling against the force of the wind.)

The final, and most drastic, method of collapsing the canopy is to use the canopy releases. This should only be used if all the previous methods have been ineffectual and should not be employed until after you have touched down.

Emergency landings

There are, of course, other landings that must be considered and these are those of an abnormal or emergency nature. The first are those landings which by necessity must be taken on hard surfaces (runways, etc.) and high wind landings (the latter being caused by a sudden increase in wind speed *during* your descent, since you should not be jumping outside the prescribed limits).

In such a situation all you can do is to adopt a really compact parachuting position, as described already, with the emphasis on keeping your feet and knees tightly together, your elbows tucked in and your chin pressed firmly down onto your chest—resist any tendency to tense up, which will be your natural instinct. More often than not you will find the landing easier than you expected simply because you have been concentrating more than usual on the correct parachute landing position. If, alternatively, you find yourself having to land into the side of a building the drill is very much the same, with the obvious difference that you should try to turn either the canopy or your body so that the first points of contact are the rounded shoulder and tucked-in elbow. Whatever you do, do not reach out towards the vertical surface with either your feet or arms as they will do no good whatsoever other than giving you possible injury.

Tree landings
Tree landings are not usually as hazardous as they sound because your rate of descent will generally be slowed as you first go into and break the thin outer branches before reaching the more solid parts of the tree. Again, the position of touch down is important, though slightly different to that which you have already learnt. Emphasis should be made on keeping your legs tightly together to prevent the painful possibility of landing astride a solid branch. Additionally, your elbows should be tucked well forwards, with your hands on your helmet to protect your face. Your

55

Tree landing position.

High tension wires landing position.

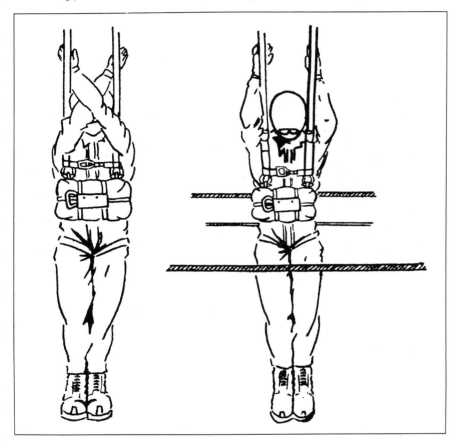

club arrive suitably equipped to extract you from the tree.

High tension cables
Landing on high tension cables is obviously a horrifying prospect and that is why parachuting regulations insist that student drop zones are located well away from any form of high tension cables. However, if a landing on high tension cables is inevitable it is essential you do everything you can to avoid the possibility of touching two wires simultaneously; if you just glance off one you might get away with it. The idea, therefore, is to make your body as straight as possible with your arms raised above your head and the palms of your hands placed against the inside of the front risers. The only other point worth making here is that if you are drifting towards high tension cables it may be possible to run downwind over them, albeit you are than faced with the possibility of a hard downwind landing; this, however, is preferable to being fried!

Water landing
The last abnormal landing is the unintentional water landing (as opposed to an intentional one which is described later). Once again, sport parachuting regulations do not allow student parachuting within a mile of open water unless all parachutists are

eyes are particularly vulnerable in this case so close them just before going into the tree. Hold the position until your descent comes to an end, resisting the temptation to grab branches as you pass by. More than likely your canopy snagging in the branches will be

what actually stops your vertical descent. If you are left hanging some distance from the ground it may be possible to use the reserve parachute as a type of rope to get down the last few feet, but if there is any doubt at all then it is safest to sit tight until other members of the

suitably equipped with an inflatable life jacket. Therefore, unintentional water landings are only likely in exceptional circumstances, e.g. leaving an aircraft in an emergency over an expanse of water. However, once you realise a water landing is inevitable the following is the drill:

1 Undo the reserve tie-down on one side and unhook the reserve parachute on the same side.
2 Undo the chest strap.
3 Using both hands, force the seat strap forwards under your backside so that you are sitting in it.
4 Cross your right hand in front of your face and firmly grasp the left-hand risers.
5 Undo both leg straps with your left hand.

6 Grasp the right-hand risers firmly with your left hand.
7 Hang on tightly in this position until your feet actually touch the water; then straighten your body sharply and throw your arms straight up above your head. This action will allow you to sink below the harness and you should now swim well clear of the main canopy.

The danger in this situation is becoming entangled with the lines or canopy, but once you are clear from your equipment you are then faced with the problem of staying afloat particularly if you are some distance from dry land. First remove your jump suit and boots, the latter, if they are parachute boots, can be tied together with the laces and

hung around your neck to provide temporary buoyancy. Your trousers, with knots tied in the ends of the legs and filled with air, can also be used as temporary water wings, as can your helmet if carefully held to trap air. Whatever you are able to do will only be of a temporary nature and it is important you try not to panic but simply apply the methods of trying to keep afloat as calmly as you can and wait for the pick up . . .

This section concludes everything you need to be taught and practise before your first descent; the remainder of the book is devoted to your progression in the sport once you have made the decision to continue.

10. Alternative methods of basic parachute training

In recent years two alternative systems of basic parachute training have been developed and some clubs are now offering these facilities. These systems are called AFF (Accelerated Freefall) and TANDEM jumping.

A tandem jump after canopy deployment.

Accelerated freefall

Accelerated freefall is the facility to make the first parachute jump a freefall descent from at least 10,000 ft. In this system the training is very much more on a one-to-one basis and the exit from the aircraft, straight into freefall, is made with an instructor holding on to each side of your harness. Two instructors will then guide you through the freefall phase of the descent correcting any small faults in body position if and when they occur. During the first descent you will also practise going

A tandem jump.

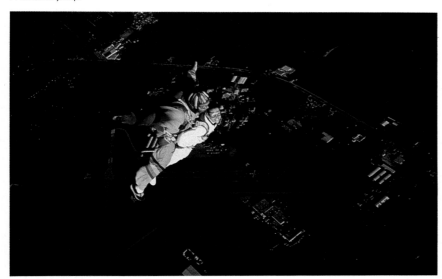

through the motions of pulling the reserve ripcord handle. Finally, of course, you will be required to activate the opening sequence by correctly using the ripcord handle and, if you should fail to do so, then one of the instructors will do it for you. Accelerated freefall has one major advantage over the static line system which is that the student is immediately exposed to the exhilaration of the freefall phase of the descent. It is, however, a more expensive method of training simply because of the one-to-one instruction basis and because the descents are made from higher altitudes.

Tandem jumping

TANDEM jumping is another alternative system that has still to be fully evaluated in many areas. In simple terms the student parachutist is attached with a harness to the front of his instructor's harness and the two will exit the aircraft together. The student and instructor descend under the same parachute which, because it is carrying double the normal weight, will obviously be much larger and bulkier. Again, this system has the advantage of exposing the student to the freefall phase of the descent right from the start.

The A.F.F. student 'dirt dives' with his instructor.

11. Parachute packing and maintenance

It is not imperative that you learn how to pack a parachute or maintain it before you carry out your first parachute descent, but if you are to continue in the sport it is vital you do so, particularly if you are to invest a large sum of money in purchasing your own parachute assembly. Obviously this does not mean that you should not take just as much trouble over the maintenance and packing of club equipment, but it does follow that the more you look after your parachuting equipment the more it will look after you.

Even when transporting parachutes it is best to keep them in proper parachute bags to avoid chafing, staining, corrosion and other evils which may be caused by leaving parachute equipment around in either the house or the boot of a car. Oil, grease and acid are particular enemies of nylon and appropriate precautions should always be taken. Avoid placing heavy objects on top of your equipment—the bending of ripcord pins and damage to ripcord housings could be possible consequences. Keep your parachutes away from strong heat; this includes direct sunlight as ultra-violet rays adversely affect nylon. If you leave your kit in the sun it is a simple matter to cover it with your jump suit or, better still, to replace it in your parachute bag. Additionally,

do not let anyone smoke anywhere near your equipment, particularly when it is laid out during the packing phase, as a cigarette burn will be expensive to repair. Finally, keep your equipment dry and aired.

After you have made your first or subsequent successful parachute landing, it will be necessary to carry your equipment back to the club. The normal method is simplicity itself. Simply lay out the parachute in a straight line away from you without removing any of your equipment. Hold out your arms in a 'sleep-walking' fashion, then bend down and, swinging your body from left to right, 'figure of eight' the parachute over your outstretched arms, first the rigging lines, then the canopy and finally the pilot-chute. When you have returned to the club or packing area lay out the parachute on the table or on the ground by allowing it to fall off your outstretched arms in reverse order: pilot-chute, canopy and rigging lines. Now you can remove the rest of your equipment. A word of warning here: if you are going to leave the parachute unpacked make sure it is visibly evident as being in this state in case it is mistaken for an assembly that is ready for jumping.

You may pack the parachute on any relatively smooth surface, ideally a proper packing table or short dry grass, or simply a clean

floor. There should be a means of securing the canopy at the apex: a hook at the end of the packing table or a stake hammered into the grass. At the other end there should again be a securing point for the 'tensioning device', which is a means of applying tension to the stretched-out parachute. The left-hand and right-hand pairs of connector links are placed over the two vertical tongues on the tensioning device before tension is applied by tightening the webbing strap. The other pieces of packing kit that are required are a 'line separator', which is a metal device with a vertical piece with two vertical slots that keep the two sets of rigging lines apart and tidy during the packing sequence; 'packing weights', which are simply bags full of lead shot or sand to keep the canopy tidy during packing; and the 'pull-up cord' and spare elastic bands. It is not possible to describe the method of packing for every single type of parachute but the basic principles remain the same, the most important being that the success of the opening of the parachute is directly proportional to the care with which it is packed in the first place.

A parachute packing hall.

Principles and packing sequence

The following principles apply to the packing of all types of parachutes:

1 Any tangles should be removed from the lines.

2 The canopy should be checked for any inversion that may have occurred when it collapsed during the landing phase. (An inversion is simply when the canopy has been turned inside out.)

3 If the canopy is wet (you might have jumped in rain) it is essential that it is hung up and dried at this stage.

4 During the packing phase the equipment should be checked for any kind of damage, and this should of course be rectified before the packing sequence is continued.

Packing square parachutes on the grass.

5 The packing sequence consists of the canopy being laid on the ground, in the case of round parachutes with the front of the canopy on the ground and the rear uppermost, and in the case of square canopies, on their side.

6 Round canopies are packed under tension, square canopies are not, but in both cases care must be taken to pleat correctly the canopy neatly and tidily.

7 The canopy is then stowed in the canopy deployment device, whether it be sleeve, bag or diaper.

8 The lines are stowed neatly in a zig-zag fashion in elastic bands, which are located on the sleeve, bag or diaper for this purpose.

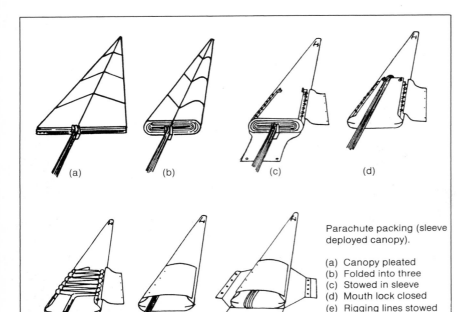

Parachute packing (sleeve deployed canopy).

(a) Canopy pleated
(b) Folded into three
(c) Stowed in sleeve
(d) Mouth lock closed
(e) Rigging lines stowed
(f) Protector flap closed
(g) Positioned in pack tray

Having looked at the basic principles you are best advised to rely on a practical demonstration and experience to learn parachute packing—there are simply too many types to learn packing from the pages of a book. There are, however, two points that can be emphasised:

Line check
This is a most important part of the packing sequence. If the lines are clear there is every chance the canopy will deploy, however scruffily you pack it. However, if the lines are not clear you have an instant malfunction. In the case of a flat circular 28-foot canopy with 28

9 The canopy inside the sleeve bag or diaper is now stowed neatly in the open pack tray.

10 The container is closed, using the pull-up cord to pull the pack closure loop through the grommets on the container flaps.

11 The whole assembly is tidied up and checked once again for any damage, particularly on the pack and harness.

12 The relevant packing card is signed by a qualified packer.

'Figure of eight' the lines to carry the parachute off the drop zone.

The standard packing checks.

Pleating the square canopy

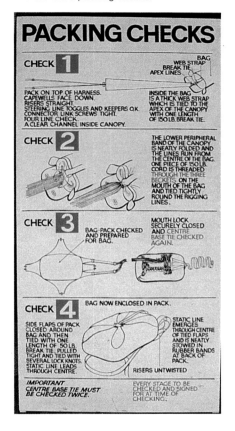

PACKING CHECKS

CHECK 1

PACK ON TOP OF HARNESS.
CAPEWELLS FACE DOWN.
RISERS STRAIGHT.
STEERING LINE TOGGLES AND KEEPERS O.K.
CONNECTOR LINK SCREWS TIGHT.
FOUR LINE CHECK.
A CLEAR CHANNEL INSIDE CANOPY.

BAG
WEB STRAP
BREAK TIE
APEX LINES

INSIDE THE BAG IS A THICK WEB STRAP WHICH IS TIED TO THE APEX OF THE CANOPY WITH ONE LENGTH OF 150 LB. BREAK TIE.

CHECK 2

THE LOWER PERIPHERAL BAND OF THE CANOPY IS NEATLY FOLDED AND THE LINES RUN FROM THE CENTRE OF THE BAG. ONE PIECE OF 150 LB. CORD IS THREADED THROUGH THE THREE BECKETS ON THE MOUTH OF THE BAG AND TIED TIGHTLY ROUND THE RIGGING LINES.

CHECK 3

BAG PACK CHECKED AND PREPARED FOR BAG.

MOUTH LOCK SECURELY CLOSED AND CENTRE BASE TIE CHECKED AGAIN.

CHECK 4

BAG NOW ENCLOSED IN PACK.

SIDE FLAPS OF PACK CLOSED AROUND BAG AND THEN TIED WITH ONE LENGTH OF 50 LB. BREAK TIE, PULLED TIGHT AND TIED WITH SEVERAL LOCK KNOTS. STATIC LINE LEADS THROUGH CENTRE.

STATIC LINE EMERGES THROUGH CENTRE OF TIED FLAPS AND IS NEATLY STOWED IN RUBBER BANDS AT BACK OF PACK.

RISERS UNTWISTED

IMPORTANT
CENTRE BASE TIE MUST BE CHECKED TWICE.

EVERY STAGE TO BE CHECKED AND SIGNED FOR AT TIME OF CHECKING.

lines, hold the left 14 rigging lines loosely in the left hand, and the right 14 rigging lines loosely in the right hand, and move up towards the canopy. When you reach the lower peripheral band, pull your hands apart until there is one gore's

Folding the canopy into the diaper on a free fall assembly.

Stowing the lines.

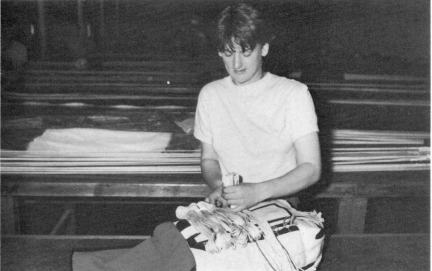

width between them. This will expose the top centre gore (the master gore—lines 1 and 28) and the bottom centre gore—lines 14 and 15. Now take lines 1 and 14 in the left hand and 15 and 28 in the right hand and glide your hands down the lines to the connector links. The lines should be clear as follows: line 1 direct to the inside top left connector link, line 14 direct to the inside of the bottom left connector link, line 28 direct to the inside of the top right connector link, and line 15 direct to the inside of the bottom right connector link. The line check will show that all the

Stowing the lines.

lines are clear and in the correct order if the four principal lines, 1, 14, 15 and 28, are clear.

Inspecting equipment
Once the lines are clear you are now ready to pack the parachute. During the packing sequence you should get into the habit of inspecting your equipment thoroughly for any faults. When you purchase the equipment initially, a thorough inspection should be made by a qualified instructor or qualified rigger. After that it is your responsibility to spot any faults and, no matter how minor they may appear, point them out to your instructor or club rigger right away. Be systematic about your inspection; the following is given as a guide.

Starting at the top, the pilot-chute should be checked for holes, tears and loose stitching. The spring should not be noticeably weak and should be securely attached to the pilot-chute. The bridle line should be untwisted, not worn, and should be securely tied to the sleeve with a bow-line knot. A bow-line should also be used to attach the sleeve retaining line to the sleeve and to the loop at the bottom of the bridle line. The top and bottom of the sleeve are likely spots for damage, so check them carefully for tears

and loose stitching. The canopy should be checked for sears, tears and burns (remember, nylon rubbing against nylon can cause burn), especially the top 3 or 4 ft from the apex, which is the 'pressure' area—so called because it suffers the greatest stress, or highest air pressure, during canopy deployment. Stains of oil, grease, acid, etc. should also be detected and neutralised on advice from your instructor or club rigger. The rigging lines should be checked for fraying or burning, and all hardware should be checked for corrosion, cracking, bending, etc. Every so often check

that the screws in the connector links are tightly done up. The pack and harness should be checked for chafing, worn stitching, straining and tears. Eventually, all these little checks will become second nature but they are, nonetheless, an important part of parachute packing.

Different types of parachute require slightly different packing methods even though the basic principles remain the same. You should, therefore, ensure that you either follow the manufacturer's instructions to the letter, or have your packing checked by an

Line stowage complete.

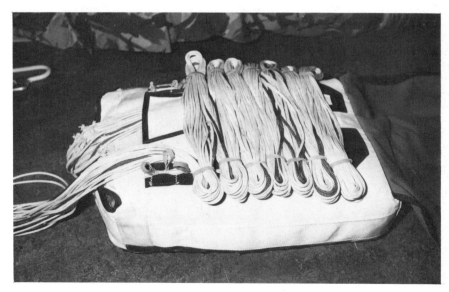

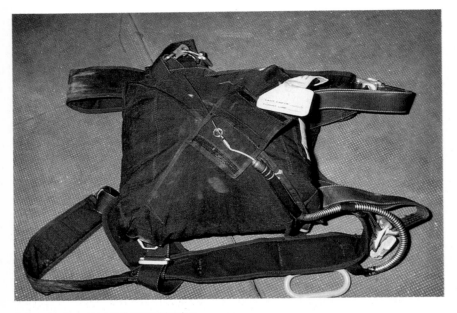

A one pin student freefall assembly after
repack complete with packing check tab.

instructor who is familiar with your
particular parachute. It is essential
that the reserve parachute is
re-packed at not more than three-
monthly intervals and the
re-packing date recorded and
signed on the packing card.

At this stage it is worth pointing
out that almost every club has a
qualified rigger on strength. Do not
be slow in approaching your club
rigger if there is any part of your
parachuting equipment that gives
cause for concern. Finally,
remember that a safe parachutist is
a careful parachutist and this is
often reflected in the way he packs
his parachute. Take a pride in your
parachute packing and be
meticulous over the maintenance of
all your equipment.

12. Student progression

Telemeter observation of student performance.

Unless you have been trained using the accelerated freefall method you will progress to become an experienced parachutist by being guided through a progression system by your instructor. The BPA category system is a proven and safe method of progression and while your natural enthusiasm may make you want to progress faster, be guided by your instructor. His total concern will be for your safe progression. Each step of this particular system will now be examined in detail.

Category 1
A requirement is that you have been passed out on basic ground training (six hours minimum) and that you are ready for your first static line descent.

This is straightforward and the initial training programme has already been outlined. Once your instructor is satisfied that you are fully trained, both mentally and physically for your very first parachute jump, he will sign you up for Category 1 on your newly acquired category card.

Category 2
(From 2,500 ft AGL)
Requirement 1: has performed a minimum of two absolutely stable observed static line descents in the full spread position counting throughout. Requirement 2: has completed a total of 13 hours of ground training in accordance with the BPA minimum ground training programme.

Both these requirements have been covered in earlier sections. Again, once they have been completed your instructor can sign up your category card, as he will do for the successful completion of each subsequent category.

Category 3
(From 2,500 ft AGL)
The requirement here is the achieving of a minimum of three successful consecutive, observed static line descents with dummy ripcord (counting throughout).

This requirement is straightforward and it simply demonstrates to your instructor that when the time comes for your first freefall descent, you are capable of

pulling the ripcord handle yourself because you have successfully done this during your Category 3 static line jumps using a dummy ripcord handle. The freefall phase of the descent is similar to the two you have already achieved as a Category 2 parachutist, with the essential difference that you are actually going through the motions of pulling the ripcord, with the main parachute still being static-line operated. Before you emplane, a dummy ripcord handle will be placed in the pocket on the harness and ideally you will have had a comprehensive practice session in a suspended harness to perfect the drills. The count is exactly the same as for Category 2 but the actions are slightly different. *One thousand* . . . force yourself into the basic spread position on exit from the aircraft. It is essential you hit this position instantly. *Two thousand* . . . glance down at the handle (without bending your head forwards) and simultaneously bring both hands into the position of the pull, with the right hand actually grasping the dummy handle. (Left hand above the head, right hand on the handle.) *Three thousand* . . . thrust out your arms to the original stable position with the dummy handle still grasped firmly in the right hand. *Four thousand* . . . check . . . exactly the same as before but after the check ensure that you secure the dummy

ripcord handle by either placing it over your wrist or stuffing it down the front of your jumpsuit before reaching up and grasping the toggles.

The dummy ripcord pull is bound to be a little unrealistic as the canopy deployment sequence is well underway before you have actually pulled the dummy handle; but you must avoid the tendency to hurry the pull and have the handle out before the canopy is deployed. The secret of a good dummy ripcord pull is twofold: first hit a really good stable position at 'one thousand' and, secondly, ensure a good recovery to the stable position on 'three thousand'. The dummy ripcord pull is not easy and you will only achieve this category by plenty of practice on the ground and by concentrating on the exact drills before and after exit from the aeroplane.

Category 4
(5-second delay—from 2,800 ft AGL)
There are four requirements in this category. 1: that you have achieved a minimum of three stable five-second delayed openings (counting throughout). 2: you have remained stable throughout opening on each descent. 3: you have looked at the ripcord handle before and during the 'reach and pull'. 4: you have achieved reasonable canopy handling.

You will almost certainly find that your first five-second delay (your first freefall) is even more memorable than your first parachute descent because now you really are on your own. Once again it is important to practise the drills on the ground in a suspended harness and these are as follows: *Go... one thousand...* hit the stable position as before, *two thousand... three thousand... four thousand...* glance down at the handle (without bending your head forwards) and simultaneously bring both hands into the position of the pull with the right hand grasping the handle, left hand above your head. *Pull thousand...* thrust out your arms, recovering to the original position with the handle being pulled out firmly by your right hand, *one thousand... two thousand... three thousand... check.*

Retain the recovered stable position until the check, then, all being well, secure the ripcord handle as already described.

The common tendency is to rush the count and in some cases to forget all that has been learnt about the stable position from the static line phase of the progression. Simply concentrate on what you are going to do before exiting the aircraft, and after exit demonstrate to your instructor a good position and let him hear a strong determined count. If at any stage of

the delay you feel yourself becoming unstable or out of control, do not hesitate—*pull the main ripcord handle immediately.*

The final requirement of Category 4 is the achieving of reasonable canopy handling and, as you will have carried out at least 8 parachute descents at this stage, you should have reached this simple standard. Neither must you forget that now that you have progressed to freefall, you are no longer dependent on a static-line deployed parachute in the event of having to abandon the aircraft in an emergency. You may therefore have to use the reserve parachute.

Category 5
(10-second delays from 3,200 ft AGL)
The two requirements in this category are as follows:
1 That you have performed a minimum of three stable 10-second delayed openings (counting throughout).
2 You have learnt to maintain heading during exit and in freefall.

Here again you will practise the drills on the ground in the suspended harness. The important thing to remember is that by the time you have fallen for 10 seconds you will have accelerated to near terminal velocity (which is normally reached after about 12 seconds of freefall) because the faster you fall,

the more dramatic will be the effect of small movements of your arms and legs on your basic stability.

The actions are the same as for Category 4 but the count is obviously longer. You will now exit the aircraft at 3,200 ft. *Go... one thousand...* hit the stable position ... *two thousand...* etc ... to *eight thousand... nine thousand...* look for and grasp the handle, having adopted the position of the pull ... *pull thousand...* the pull and the recovery to the stable position ... *one thousand... two thousand... three thousand... check.*

The requirement to maintain heading during freefall is not a difficult one to achieve. If your exit has been a good one you will be facing in the same direction as the aircraft is flying. After exit you can glance down at the ground and ensure that you are not turning either to left or right. If you find that you are, the turn can be corrected by gently leaning in the opposite direction. Once you are back on heading, you should straighten into your original stable position. But as before, if you have any tendency towards loss of control or a turn which you cannot stop right away, you must operate the main ripcord handle immediately no matter at what height you are.

Category 6

(15-second delays from 4,000 ft AGL)

The required performance for this category is a minimum of three flat stable delayed openings in the following sequence:

1 One flat stable delayed opening counting throughout.

2 After introduction to instruments, two flat stable delayed openings with instruments but continuing to count throughout.

During these three descents a strong position is required on exit and for the first 6 seconds, and then a more relaxed position may be assumed with aircraft heading maintained throughout.

This is another important step in your training for after 15 seconds of freefall your terminal velocity will be about 120 mph. Therefore, you will find that any movement of your limbs will more readily upset or alter your basic stability—in fact, having reached terminal velocity, you will have gained a more positive control in freefall. The first descent in this category is simply designed to take you through the attainment of terminal velocity without any additional manoeuvres. The pull is initiated on *four thousand* . . . activated on *pull thousand* . . . and carried through to the check after *three thousand* in the normal way.

The second part of the requirement introduces the use of

A P.I.S.A. 26′ Lo Po reserve canopy.

the altimeter in addition to the normal verbal count. On the climb to altitude in the aircraft you will notice the needle of your altimeter (the latter normally being mounted on the top of your reserve parachute) moving steadily around the dial until it reaches the jump altitude of 4,000 ft (having been set to zero on the ground). To read the altimeter in freefall is simply a matter of glancing down at it at frequent intervals; do not bend the head right forward and resist any tendency to relax your stable position. You should initiate the pull when the altimeter reads 2,300 ft, which should coincide with your count of *fourteen thousand*. If your count reaches fourteen thousand before the altimeter reads 2,300 ft, then pull; you may have rushed your count but this isn't the time to work it out. Likewise, if the altimeter unwinds to 2,300 ft before your count of *fourteen thousand* you should pull immediately for the same reasons. An altimeter is a mechanical device and so, of course, it is possible that it may malfunction. You will have become used to what 2,000 ft looks like at this time and it should be your back-up in event of altimeter failure. The important drill, however, is that if in doubt activate your main ripcord handle immediately.

71

Simple body turn to the left.

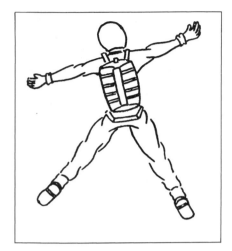

Category 7
(20-second delays from 5,000 ft AGL)

The performance required here is a minimum of four 20-second delayed opening descents in the following sequence:

1 One 20-second delayed opening, maintaining aircraft heading and continuing to count throughout and relaxing the position.

2 One 20-second delayed opening with a 360° left turn after a 10-second fall away stopping on aircraft heading.

3 One 20-second delayed opening with a 360° right turn after a 10-second fall away stopping on aircraft heading.

4 One 20-second delayed opening, with precise alternate turns left and right.

The 20-second category has two basic aims:

1 To reduce the body position, with a re-emphasis on the importance of trim to ensure that the jumper can fall absolutely vertically, and

2 the rotation of the upper body and arms as one unit downwards (about 15–20°) in the direction of the desired turn and leaning gently into the turn. The turn should be stopped by opposite rotation and then the neutral position as the

heading comes up again. Once again, these turns will be practised in the suspended harness and the importance of pulling immediately if the turn cannot be corrected must be stressed.

Category 8
(30 and 35 seconds from 7,000 and 8,000 ft AGL respectively)

The requirement here is the performance of a minimum of eight descents of 30- and 35-second delays in the following sequence:

1 One unstable exit with alternate turns with precision.

2 One unstable exit with backloops.

3 One dive exit with backloops.

4 Two tracks.

5 Two track turns (sharp 45–90° left or right as an avoiding manoeuvre while maintaining the track).

6 One half-series with short track and wave off from a minimum altitude of 8,000 ft AGL and, finally,

7 Cleared for self spotting descents up to 8,000 ft AGL.

The recovery from the unstable exit is an enjoyable experience. On exit from the aircraft initiate a three-second tumble with your arms around your knees, and then arch hard. The effect of this will be to move you instantly into a traditional stable position. Backloops and tracking will be examined in the next section. Suffice to say here that a half-series is simply a 360° turn in alternate directions followed by a backloop. Spotting (the art of leaving the aircraft in the right place) will be discussed in some detail later but, of course, it is important that before you are able to parachute without supervision you must learn this art to ensure that you leave the aeroplane in the right placé and land on the target in the middle of the drop zone.

On completion of the dive exit and backloops the student may be introduced to a tandem system with throw-away pilot-chute and high-performance round canopy. The tandem system is where the reserve is mounted above the main on the back and so it is essential that cut-away drills are taught and practised

72

before the use of this system. A throw-away pilot-chute is an alternative method of canopy deployment to activation by ripcord handle. In this case the pilot-chute is stowed in a pocket outside the main container and is simply pulled into the slipstream by the parachutist and the deploying throw-away pilot-chute pulls open the pack and the deployment sequence continues in the normal way.

On completion of Category 8 and a minimum of five tandem system jumps you may well be recommended to use a ram air canopy by your instructor who will then endorse your log book. Prior to this first ram-air descent a formal brief will be given by your instructor, which will include revision on the tandem emergency procedures.

Both Category 9 and Category 10 are designed to finish off your student training and take you through a programme of relative work parachuting which will allow you to qualify as an 'experienced' parachutist. Relative work training is covered in a separate section and, therefore, it is only necessary at this stage to lay down the basic requirements.

Category 9

The requirement is for the introduction to relative work parachuting and the following

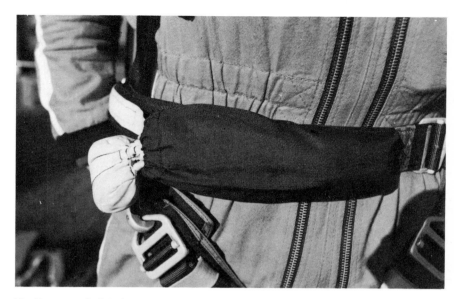

The 'throwaway' pilot-chute stowage.

instructional relative work exercises to have been carried out:
1 Fast fall, slow fall.
2 Horizontal movement, forwards / backwards.
3 Sideslip left and right.
4 Back-ins.
5 Side-ins.
6 360° flat turns left and right, and levelling.
In this category it is recommended that instruction groups be two persons only, i.e. ideally student and instructor.

Category 10

There are only three requirements here:
1 One pin, backloop, pin. (The 'pin' is the ability to close and join up with another parachutist in free fall.)
2 One close third.
3 One close fourth.
Once you have achieved all these

categories and they have been signed up in your log book by your instructor, you may consider yourself to be an 'experienced' parachutist. It would be ridiculous, however, to consider that the attainment of Category 10 is the end of your learning situation. Nothing could be further from the truth, with every subsequent parachute descent making you a safer and more experienced parachutist.

13. Ram-air canopies

Introduced in the early 1970s the ram-air canopy has proved to be one of the sport's most important innovations. The canopy is rectangular in plan and has an aerofoil cross section, thus making it look very like an inflated wing. This aerofoil cross section is kept inflated by having the leading edge open. The airflow is forced into the front of the canopy during deployment, thereby keeping it rigid throughout the descent. The deployment device on the ram-air canopy is known as a 'slider'. It is simply a reinforced square of nylon about 18 inches by 18 inches with a large (number 8) grommet in each corner. One set of lines from each riser passes through each of the four grommets. When the canopy has been packed the slider is pulled to the top of the lines before the latter are stowed in the bag, and during deployment it slides down the lines allowing an acceptable and gradual inflation of the canopy.

As the ram-air canopy is basically an inflatable wing it is subject to much the same forces as those inherent on an aeroplane's wing. There are numerous types of ram-air canopy available on the market. Most have seven inflatable cells and a wing area of some 250 sq. ft, with the canopy weighing about 7–8 lb. They have a minimum rate of

The 'GQ Unit'—a typical 7-cell ram-air canopy.

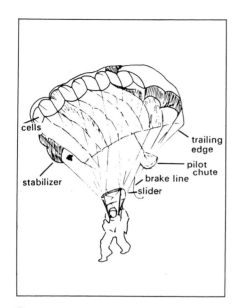

cells

trailing edge

pilot chute

stabilizer

brake line

slider

The ram-air canopy—in this case, a Strato-Flyer.

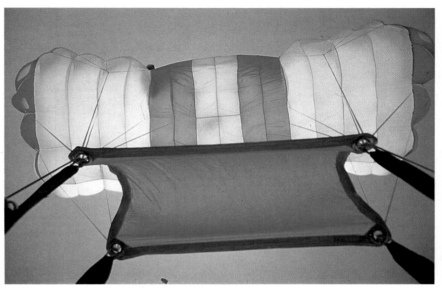

The jumper's view of the inflated 7-cell canopy and 'slider'.

descent of about 5 feet per second (from a 'flared' landing) and a maximum forward speed of about 25 mph. You can readily see, therefore, why it is important that landings with ram-air canopies are made, as aircraft, facing into wind. One problem of the ram-air canopy is its inherent fast forward speed which necessitates the brakes being applied during packing—various methods are in use. After canopy deployment the brakes must be released but not before checking that you are well clear of other canopies in the sky. Initial steering to avoid canopy collision, with the brakes still applied, may be achieved by pulling down on either of the rear risers to achieve a turn in that direction. Because of its

A 7-cell ram-air canopy from below on half-brakes.

inherent high performance the ram-air canopy can be very difficult to handle in a malfunctioned state with any asymmetric profile and

may cause alarmingly fast rotations. If this should happen the cut-away drill should be initiated without delay.

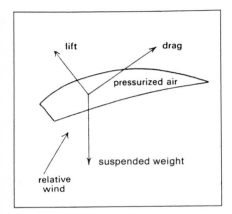

Forces acting on a ram-air canopy in flight.

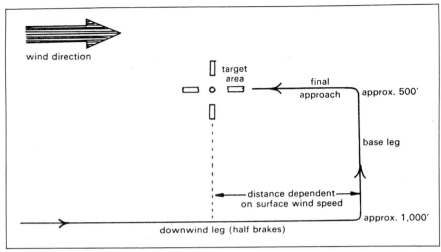

The ram-air canopy approach.

Any ram-air canopy will come complete with a very extensive manual and it should be studied in detail before making your first descent on the new canopy (this is why only generalisations are made here). The flying of the canopy is normally done with half brakes, with your hands held well in front of you so you can see their relative position. It is important with the ram-air canopy to minimise the amount of toggle movement, particularly close to the ground. When approaching the target area with a ram-air canopy ignore the wind-cone, but take into account the wind line and, of course, the wind speed. The pattern flown during the latter part of the descent is identical to that which an aircraft uses on its approach to land. A downwind leg is flown parallel with

the wind line past the target (how far past is dependent on the wind speed, and experience will be the ultimate guide). At about 1,000 ft a right-angled turn is made towards the wind line, followed by a further right-angled turn into wind on the wind line at about 500 ft.

Throughout the approach the canopy should be flown on half brakes—precision ram-air approaches are discussed later. A normal landing with a ram-air canopy is the 'flared' landing. Again, this is similar to landing in an aircraft, the idea being to touch down at the slowest forward speed possible, combined with the slowest rate of descent just above the canopy stall. At about 20 ft up from the half-brake position the canopy is flared for landing by pulling both toggles firmly down to arm's length.

The reaching of this arm's length position should actually coincide with your touch down. It should be practised slowly at first because if you reach the stall position just above the ground it will have disastrous results with the canopy simply falling out of the sky. On your early ram-air jumps the stall characteristics of the canopy should be experienced in detail at altitude, with the positions of your hands on the toggles being noted carefully.

In the early days of jumping a ram-air canopy treat it with infinite respect as it can be likened to a thoroughbred horse or high performance sports car—if handled incorrectly it can have disastrous results.

14. Freefall manoeuvres

The aim of this section is to explain the essential principles of performing the various freefall manoeuvres that are the basic skills of your sport parachuting progression. Three simple rules are relevant before looking at individual descriptions.

1 It is important to practise all these manoeuvres in the suspended harness on the ground first.

2 When you are sitting in the aircraft on the climb to altitude concentrate on what you are actually going to do in freefall, so that you do not have to give it a second thought after exit from the aircraft.

3 All freefall manoeuvres are initiated and achieved by the movement of some or all of your limbs, which either vary the effective surface area of your body, shift your centre of gravity or cause deflection of the flow of air past your body. These parameters play an important part in the execution of the manoeuvres.

The first freefall manoeuvre to be considered is the variation of the basic stable position to either increase or decrease the vertical rate of descent. These positions can be called fast fall and slow fall.

Fast fall and slow fall

The ability to vary one's vertical rate of descent is important in the execution of relative work parachuting, but more of that later. All that is necessary at this stage is to understand the simple principles. The fast fall position is merely a closing up of the stable position where the hands, arms and legs should be pulled in closer to the body. The speed with which this is executed will obviously affect the rate of initiation of the fast fall. The recovery works in a similar way, with a resumption to your relaxed stable position. The tighter the position, the faster you will fall.

The slow fall is exactly the opposite, with an increase in surface area being caused by extending the spreading of the arms and legs which will increase your drag and thus decrease your rate of descent. Both fast and slow fall should be assumed slowly, and can be practised by moving gently from one to the other. Do not waste more than one descent on practising this solo, but wait until you can execute it with an instructor or experienced parachutist falling alongside you: this will give you an idea of how effective your variations in rate of descent are in practice.

Back to earth stable position

This is the next manoeuvre. Practice of it is not vital to your progression but it is an enjoyable exercise to prepare yourself for the disorientated feeling you will surely experience when you first lose visual contact with the earth. This may occur at any time during your progression, and specifically if you execute a freefall manoeuvre without the necessary aggression and make a nonsense of it. The back to earth position is exactly the opposite of the basic freefall stable position. Your back should be rounded, head pushed forwards, arms relaxed with palms facing upwards, and your legs straight and apart. Try to hold the position for a specified count in spite of the insecure feeling you will undoubtedly experience. Do not trust an altimeter in this position as

The radical back to earth position.

it is located in a partial vacuum and may not read accurately. To resume your original stable position simply force this position on as previously practised and you will flip over to see the earth spread reassuringly below you.

Turns

The simple body turn has already been described but there are other methods of speeding the turn and also initiating it with either arms or legs. Practising both these situations is a basic freefall skill. Obviously the tighter your basic body position, the faster will be the turn once you initiate it. To turn only using your arms is simply a matter of pushing down the arm on the side of your body in that direction you wish to turn. Similarly, to turn using your legs, the easiest method is to tuck in the leg on the side of

the direction you wish to go. In both cases this automatically gives increased lift on the opposite side, and is quick and efficient. If you combine these with pushing at the waist in the direction you wish to go you will also increase the speed of the turn. Again, practise all these movements in the suspended harness before trying them out in the air. Remember: when you execute turns in freefall, stop and start them on a given heading. This is important because there is little point in starting a turn if you cannot stop it accurately. You will find that only a reasonable amount of practise in freefall will enable you to execute fast precision turns which can be stopped on a given heading.

The Delta position

The Delta position provides the parachutist with a limited means of

making ground horizontally. From the basic position the legs are straightened, kept about 30° apart, and the straight arms with palms facing downwards are swept back at anything between 30° and 45°, depending on the required effectiveness of the position. The result of sweeping back the arms is to lower the head because the effective surface area of the upper part of the body has been reduced; thus the airflow tends to be directed along the underside of the body towards the feet to give a certain amount of forward displacement, and the rate of descent is increased at the same time. The more swept back the arms, the more head down the position, and thus the greater the rate of descent. The most effective horizontal displacement is achieved with the arms swept back at about 30° from the body; if they are swept back any further, the increase in vertical rate of descent and radical head down position obliterates any horizontal displacement. The extreme of this is the no-lift dive—your hands are placed alongside the body, your head is directly in line with it, and the only surface area presented to the airflow is your shoulders. In this case you will fall very fast and vertically straight downwards.

To turn in the Delta position, just move your head and upper part of your body in the direction you wish

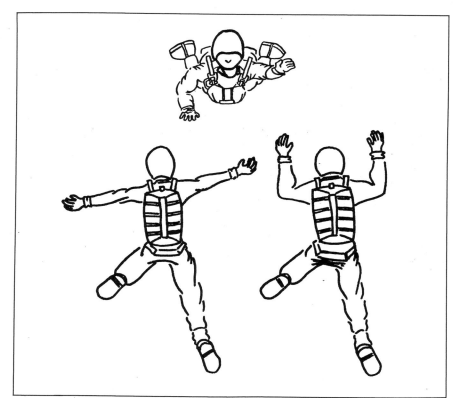

Simple body turns.

The Delta position.

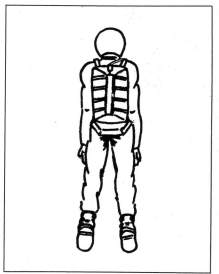

to turn. The Delta position, as you will learn later, has a number of uses but one is particularly worthy of mention at this stage and that is the recovery from the fast turn or flat spin. In the early days you will be taught that if you cannot stop a turn or spin, having briefly tried to counter it, you should activate the ripcord right away, and this teaching should always be applied below 4,000 ft anyway. However, if you have plenty of experience and height, you can use the Delta position simply to dive out of and

A no-lift dive.

recover from a spin. It is very similar to the standard spin recovery that is used in flying an aeroplane. Finally, never be persuaded to open your parachute in the Delta position, as you are travelling too fast. Always allow time to move from the Delta position back to the basic stable position well before you pull the ripcord. This important point applies even more to the next manoeuvre, which is called *tracking*.

Tracking

Tracking is the ultimate means by which the parachutist can cover distance horizontally in freefall. The tracking position may be likened to a crude aerofoil section and this is the basis of its success. The aerofoil is designed to give lift when it moves forwards through the air and in the tracking position your body is achieving maximum lift by trying to resemble the aerofoil in section. An efficient tracking position can achieve as much as 35° from the vertical. It is, however, a manoeuvre that requires considerable practice.

On exit from the aircraft, face the direction in which you wish to move, then assume a full Delta position. From that position move gradually into the tracking position by pulling in the stomach, pushing up your behind, rounding your shoulders, straightening your legs but keeping them a few inches apart, pointing

your toes and straightening your arms along your sides with the palms facing downwards; your head should be forced back against the top of the backpack. The amount of reverse arch you apply is the key to the successful track and can only be found by experimentation. Feel your way into the position slowly until you experience the exhilaration of building up lift and speed and actually feel yourself moving horizontally. The track may be finely balanced by small movements of the hands and arms. It is most frequently used when a parachutist discovers he has left the aircraft over the wrong point on the ground and then wishes to move horizontally to put himself back over the right spot before opening his parachute (it is such a basic freefall skill that it features as an important facet of the BPA category system).

You must also learn to turn in the track and this is simply achieved by digging down with the hand on the side of the direction in which you wish to turn. In recovering from the track ensure you allow plenty of time, in the first two or three jumps at least 1,000 ft, in which to decelerate before opening the main parachute.

The back loop

The execution of a backloop is not too difficult but the execution of a

fast, precise backloop requires considerable practice. It is achieved by simultaneously pushing violently forwards and downwards with the arms, pulling the knees up sharply to the chest and forcing back the head. The upper part of the body is forced upwards by the airflow and, if the loop is started vigorously enough, the momentum will carry you right over the top. As the earth comes into view again, simply flare out to your original stable position. If the manoeuvre is executed with indecision you may well roll off the top of it before completion or come out of it away from your original heading. If this should happen give yourself a mental command of 'GO!', which may assist you in starting the backloop with sufficient energy; you may find that keeping your arms and legs slightly apart will help you to remain on heading throughout.

The forward loop

The forward loop you may find more difficult. Extend your legs, keeping them apart for stability, tuck your chin onto your chest and bring your arms right in alongside your chest. Immediately bend forwards at the waist, thrusting your head downwards which will start the forward rotation. As you go over the top, tuck in your legs and push your arms out to the side to resume your

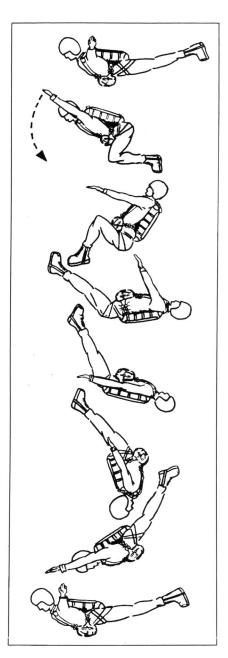

The back loop.

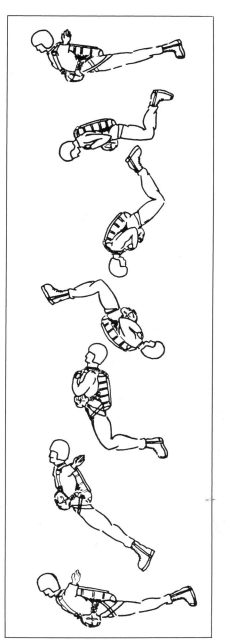

The forward loop.

original position as the earth comes into view once more.

The barrel roll

To initiate a barrel roll to the right straighten your legs, keeping them a few inches apart, and fold in the right arm across your chest. This will have the effect of turning you over to the right and onto your back; to finish the roll smoothly simply fold in your left arm over your chest and extend your right arm. You can assist the movement by twisting your body in the direction of the roll. When the earth comes into view resume your original position as before. Once again, if you do not enter the barrel roll smoothly and with some sort of vigour the roll will almost certainly go adrift. Needless to say, practice will produce a smooth barrel roll on heading.

These words and diagrams can only present basic principles. Your own individual body shape and the equipment you are wearing will also influence the execution of all these manoeuvres. Therefore, experience and practice will assist you in performing them with speed and precision: they are part of your basic skills as a freefall parachutist.

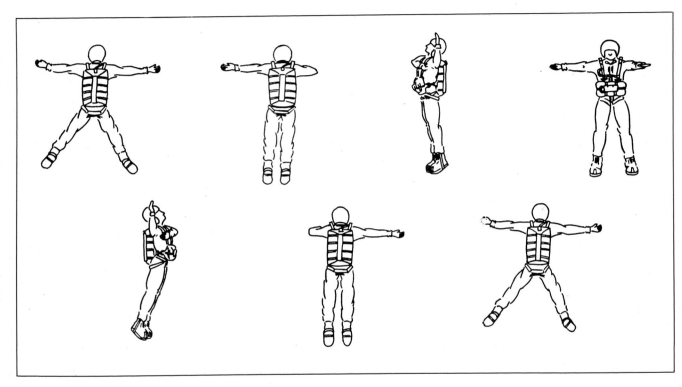

The barrel roll (to the right) (see previous
page for an explanation of the barrel roll
manoeuvre).

15. Spotting

The ability to line up the aircraft over the drop zone during its run-in and to decide at what stage you will exit it to ensure that you land at a pre-designated point on the ground is called 'spotting'. Spotting is the twofold skill of deciding theoretically where you are going to exit the aircraft and then being able to do it in practice. The principal variables are, of course, the wind speed and direction. To a lesser extent the speed of the aircraft should be considered as this also has an effect. For the theory of spotting to be understood it is necessary to divide the actual descent into three distinct phases:

1 The 'throw forward'. At the moment of exit you are travelling at the same speed as the aircraft and, therefore, for the first few seconds of your descent you are, in fact, projected forwards by the speed of the aircraft. This is the throw forward.

2 The 'freefall drift'. This is the distance you are moved across the ground by the upper winds during the freefall part of your descent.

3 'Canopy drift'. This is the part of the descent when you are drifting, or flying, under the deployed parachute.

There are two small but important definitions which should be mentioned here. The first is the

definition of 'exit point': the exit point is that point on the ground over which you actually step out of the aircraft. Second is 'opening point': this is the point on the ground over which you open your parachute to enable you to land on the pre-designated target.

Spotting from above. Typical airfield with DZ layout. Arrowed broken line shows the run-in for this example.

Canopy drift

Before take off the pilot should be briefed to fly directly over the target into wind at 2,000 ft AGL for the run to drop the WDI (wind drift indicator). This briefing is best done using the air photograph of the drop zone, which every club should

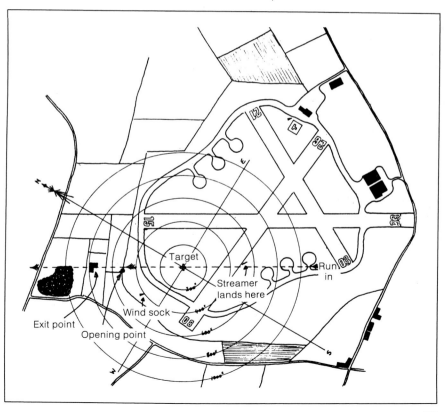

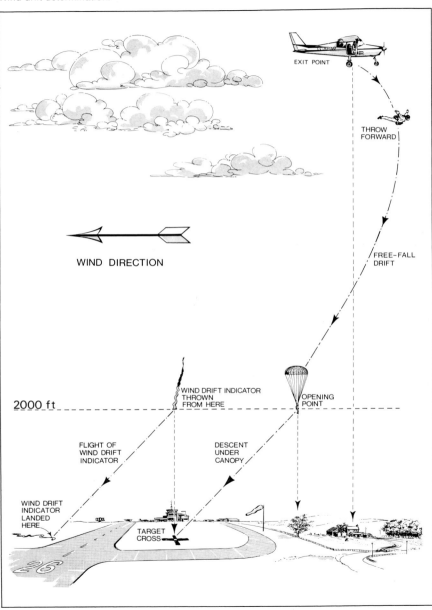

Wind drift determination.

have in its possession. Ideally the photograph should be superimposed with a transparent compass rose over the target area. Once the pilot has lined up the aircraft into wind at between 1800 and 2,200 ft it is only necessary for you to give him final corrections left and right because he cannot see straight down below the aircraft at this stage. Even this part of the exercise will take some practice as the sill of the door may not run strictly fore and aft but at an angle, which may tend to give you a false impression of the actual run-in line. Remember, if the aircraft is climbing or banking left or right you will not have a clear vertical view of the target area; it is, therefore, important that the pilot is flat and level at the moment of dropping the WDI. Signals may be passed to the pilot either verbally, visually (in a mirror) or by using a system of signal lights. Verbal corrections should give the direction first, followed by the number of degrees, i.e. 'Right ... 5'. Having given the correction let the aircraft settle on its new heading, assess the situation and then give a further correction if need be. If you do not let the aircraft settle you will not get a clear picture of the ground. Just before throwing the WDI you should unroll the first two or three feet and retain this amount in your grip, which will ensure that it unrolls immediately it is thrown into the slipstream.

When the aircraft is directly overhead the target the moment is now right to throw the WDI violently outwards and downwards and to shout 'OK' to the pilot, which is the sign for him to bank round to the side from which you have just thrown it. You must not let it out of your sight until it reaches the ground; this is often easier said than done in hazy conditions but if you lose sight of it you have no alternative but to throw another, which is just a waste of time. Once you have seen it land the point should be memorised and indicated to the pilot. The opening point is on a straight line drawn through the point where the WDI landed and the target, at the same distance the other side. If necessary now is the time to indicate the opening point to the other parachutists in the aircraft. Do not forget this opening point as you will be expected to mark it on the air photograph for everyone's benefit later. Thus canopy drift has been determined, but as the wind will also affect the jumpers in freefall this must be the next consideration.

Freefall drift

In practice jumpers seldom calculate the freefall drift but tend to guestimate it by looking at the clouds and assessing an upper wind speed and direction; this may not be all that accurate but it only needs the first aircraft load of the day to prove it one way or the other—and for casual club jumping this is normally acceptable.

Freefall drift can, of course, be calculated reasonably accurately and you should know how to do this. Remember that for the calculation 2 kts are equal to 1 metre per second (it is important to know as wind speeds will be given in knots (nautical miles per hour)). The upper wind forecast can usually be obtained from your nearest met. office and the information that you will receive should be tabulated as in the example below:

To calculate freefall drift, simply add up the freefall drift windspeed in metres and the wind direction in degrees, in this case 115 and 2510. To find the average now divide each of these totals by the number of sets of figures: here it is 8, to give 14·5 metres per second and 314°. This means that for every second of freefall, the drift is 14·5 metres from a direction of 314°. In this case there are 50 seconds of freefall (see the chart at the end of the section), so the total drift is 14·5 × 50, or 715 metres. The distance of 715 m and direction of 314° can now be plotted on the air photograph to provide the exit point. Additionally, your canopy drift can be calculated from the figures given above and

Height in feet		Speed		Direction (from which the wind is coming in degrees true)
		knots	metres/sec	
Canopy drift	Surface	8	4	260°
	1,000	10	5	270°
	2,000	12	6	270°
Free-fall drift	3,000	16	8	280°
	4,000	18	9	280°
	5,000	22	11	290°
	6,000	28	14	310°
	7,000	30	15	320°
	8,000	36	18	340°
	9,000	40	20	340°
	10,000	40	20	350°
		8\115	8\2510°	
		14½	314°	

A Cherokee 6 (PA 32) on run in for the wind drift indicator at 2000'.

occasionally this is necessary when jumping at an air show where a tight schedule does not allow for the throwing of a WDI. The procedure is the same, merely average out the three sets of figures bracketed as canopy drift and you get a result of 5 metres per second from 217° You will be hanging under your canopy for about 2 minutes; therefore, 5 metres per second for 120 seconds gives a

86

canopy drift of 600 metres. Here again this can be plotted on the air photograph to provide the opening point.

Throw forward

The final consideration is that of throw forward and more often than not it is ignored. It may be necessary to know, however, in a competition accuracy situation and a virtually no-wind condition where you will have to exit downwind of

the target to allow the throw forward from the aircraft to position you upwind for the correct opening point. It is also important when jumping out of larger aircraft with a more than normal run-in speed. Throw forward is calculated by using the formula

$$P = \frac{5VT}{T+5}$$

where P is the required throw forward in metres, V is the true

A 7-cell ram-air canopy on half-brakes.

airspeed of the aircraft in metres per second, and T is the length of delay in seconds up to a maximum of 12 (terminal velocity). An example of this might be from a Cessna 172 with a true airspeed of 65 kts (32 metres per second) on a 10 second delay.

$$P = 5 \times 32 \times \frac{10}{10} + 5 = 5 \times 32 \times$$

$$\frac{10}{15} = \frac{320}{3} = 107 \text{ metres.}$$

The exit point on the air photograph can now be adjusted accordingly.

Essentially spotting is not difficult and only requires a certain amount of practice. You will, however, be expected to spot yourself accurately (this is a qualification necessary for attainment of the BPA Category 8). The following table will give a guide to distance fallen in freefall in a stable spread position. It must, of course, only be used as a simple guide.

Distance fallen in free fall stable spread position

Caution: The rate of descent increases with (1) other body position, (2) higher temperatures, (3) lower pressure (e.g. higher field elevation). Use this table with extreme caution at field elevations over 1,000 feet, especially during long delays. Always add 100 feet extra for each 1,000 feet of field elevation.

Distance fallen each second to terminal velocity		Total distance fallen in freefall stable spread position. Distance measured in feet.									
Secs	Distance	Secs	Distance	Secs	Distance	Secs	Distance	Secs	Distance	Secs	Distance
1	16	1	16	13	1657	25	3745	37	5833	49	7921
2	46	2	62	14	1831	26	3919	38	6007	50	8095
3	76	3	138	15	2005	27	4093	39	6181	51	8269
4	104	4	242	16	2179	28	4267	40	6355	52	8443
5	124	5	366	17	2353	29	4441	41	6529	53	8617
6	138	6	504	18	2527	30	4615	42	6703	54	8791
7	148	7	652	19	2701	31	4789	43	6877	55	8965
8	156	8	808	20	2875	32	4963	44	7051	56	9139
9	163	9	971	21	3049	33	5137	45	7225	57	9313
10	167	10	1138	22	3223	34	5311	46	7399	58	9487
11	171	11	1309	23	3397	35	5485	47	7573	59	9661
12	174	12	1483	24	3571	36	5659	48	7747	60	9835

As an example, if a 20 second delay is required, look up the distance fallen against 20 seconds (in this case 2,875) and add the normal opening height of 2,000 feet; this gives 4,875 feet or 5,000 feet in round figures.

16. Relative work

Relative work may be defined as the ability two or more parachutists have to fly 'relative to each other'. Relative work has developed over the years into that branch of the sport to which most parachutists aspire. The reason for this is twofold: firstly, because it involves skydiving with one's friends, and, secondly, because it is a comparatively easily acquired skill which in turn gives the most enormous amount of fun and satisfaction in its execution. Additionally, there are only two limiting factors. The first of these is the size of the aeroplane to be used; this will obviously place restrictions on the number of parachutists who can be involved in any group flying. The second limitation is simply one of imagination; there is absolutely no end to the varied possibilities of type and size of formation or

DC3 exit for a large relative work formation.

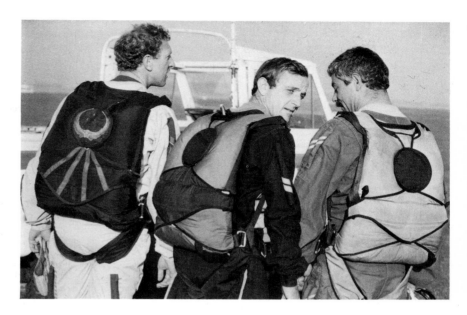

Three 'Racer' lightweight tandem assemblies—favoured equipment of relative workers.

formations that can be flown in freefall.

Relative work also has its own inherent dangers and basically these fall into two groups. First is the danger of not being aware of your altitude in freefall and getting carried away with the jump in hand; this can obviously have disastrous results. The second danger is the possibility of mid-air collisions either in freefall or after the canopy has deployed. Once you have been taught all the basics of body control and have the ability to track proficiently, you now have the essential tools for your safe introduction to relative work. Being taught relative work properly from the start will eliminate any possibility of you becoming susceptible to the dangers of this aspect of the sport through poor execution. Relative work cannot be a self-taught affair and there are no short-cuts; however, if you are taught by a qualified instructor or 'tutor' according to a proper training programme, it can be learnt to a reasonable standard over less than a dozen jumps.

Any relative work jump should be carefully pre-planned, but the briefings for your first half dozen or so must be particularly clear and comprehensive. Your instructor will tell you first what he wants *you* to do, next what he is going to do himself, thirdly the particular points

he wants you to look out for, and· finally the wave-off height and procedure. Your individual size and body weight will have an effect on the way you fly individually and you can expect your instructor to advise you personally on this. Basically, the smaller and lighter you are, the more relative work flexibility you will have, and, I suspect, the easier you will find the learning process.

'Dirt diving' is the term given to practising any relative work skydive on the ground. It involves practice of the move to and the exit from the aircraft, and the sequence of the skydive itself. Dirt diving is very much a routine of relative work and is essential in order that the entire sequence of the skydive is retained in one's memory and then acted upon vigorously in freefall. Don't be tempted either to skimp on the dirt dive or to reject it altogether, as the

resultant skydive will be adversely affected—and, therefore, a waste of money. There is no set pattern of a learning progression for relative work, but that which follows is a proven one and will rapidly progress you to a level where all the basic relative work skills have been successfully achieved. It is a sound grounding for whatever will follow.

Jump no. 1 (from 9,000 ft minimum): *To introduce surface area control.* You will exit the aircraft number one and hold a heading and relaxed position as practised on the ground beforehand. Your instructor will follow and set himself up level and face to face with you about three or four feet away. He will then vary his rate of descent by increasing or decreasing his surface area from a big de-arch position to a tight tucked-in position (ultra slow fall to

fast fall). Your task is to stay with him by simply emulating his changes in body position. He will not exceed your ability and in the initial part of the descent the changes in body position will be very gradual. If this is assimilated readily your instructor can speed up the changes. You must check your altitude and you will be expected to initiate the break-off at 3,500 ft AGL, following this with a forceful track, wave off and pull.

The maximum de-arch position is to be used when you have gone low and need to return to a safe height from which to re-start your approach. The hands are pushed down and slightly forwards. Your head must be down also because if you look up you bend your spine in the wrong direction and it will only efficiently bend in one direction at a time. So look down and then pull in your stomach and stick your backside up. Your toes and fingers should be pointed downwards. This max. de-arch position will give the slowest rate of descent possible.

Jump no. 2 (from a minimum of 9,000 ft): *To introduce lateral movement.*
Again you will exit first, followed by your instructor who will set himself up alongside you three or four feet away; both of you face the same direction. Once more the exercise is initiated by your instructor setting the move which you then follow. He will start with a gentle forward movement by gradually bringing his arms back—you stay with him. He will increase forward speed by bringing his arms back further still and straightening his legs—again you follow. The ultimate forward speed may be practised with you

both tracking side by side. After deceleration you will practise backward and sideways movements—again by following your instructor's example. As for jump no. 1, this jump will finish by you initiating the break-off.

Small changes in direction, whether they be forward, backward or sideways, are normally carried out with the arms, legs or, indeed, the whole body by the deflection of the airflow around it. For instance, if you tuck in your legs and extend your arms your head will fly higher than your feet and air deflection will tend to move you backwards. Likewise if you tend to tuck in the arm and leg on the same side of your body that side will tend to fall relative to the other, and the deflection of airflow will move you to that side in a sideslip.

Jump no. 3 (from 9,000 ft minimum): *To introduce contact formation levelling, tensionless grips and lateral motion.*
Once again you will exit first and your instructor will follow, flying to one side of you and taking a grip so that you are both facing the same way. He will then change his rate of descent and move laterally with the grip held, with you following his example to keep station with him. Be aware of any tension that develops when you don't stay with him precisely; some time during the

descent when you are flying accurately in a position of no tension, your instructor will release his grip and then take it again, showing that this need not cause lateral movement. Your instructor will finish, on an agreed signal, with a delta with the grip maintained, demonstrating faster lateral movement as a contact pair. Break-off will be as normal at 3,500 ft.

Jump no. 4 (from 9,000 ft minimum): *To introduce approaches and* *dockings using no contact, no grip flying.*

Your instructor will again follow you out and position himself about four or five feet immediately in front of you. From this position he will demonstrate moving into you,

A 3-way with one flying inverted.

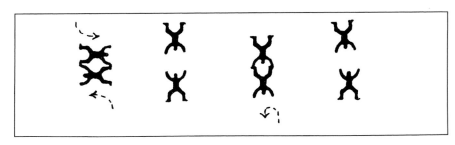

touching both your hands, but not taking a grip. He will then back away and you repeat the exercise yourself. When your hands have been overlapped for a couple of seconds, your instructor will dart away; his position this time, however, will not be directly in front of you or necessarily on the same level. You will then make a second no-contact docking by having to turn and gain or lose height in the process. This can be repeated if altitude permits before a normal break-off.

Jump no. 5 (from 9,000 ft minimum): *To introduce various docking manoeuvres.*
You will exit the aircraft after your instructor and dock straight into a 'monopole'. Follow this with an opposite monopole, a back-in to a two-man 'caterpillar' and then a 'compressed accordian', with both of you turning as the docking is completed. These formations can be carried out in any order and your instructor might also include a 'stair-step' or a 'line' for variety. The aim of this jump is for you, the student, to be in continuous motion from one formation to the next, but you should not rush it; work on flow and precision—not speed. The break-off is as already practised.

The 'back-in' or 'side-in' are docking maneouvres which sound more complicated than they in fact

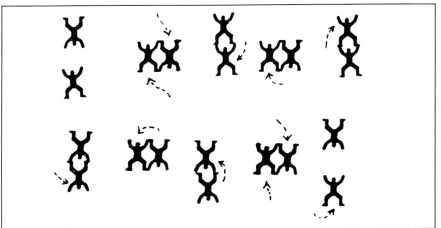

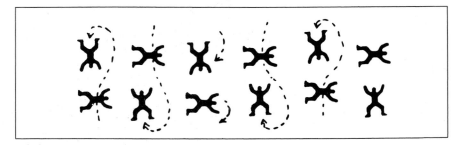

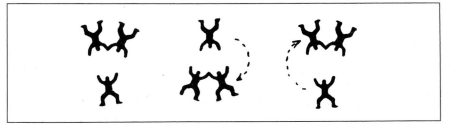

are. They are both developed from the forward momentum during the approach; a turn is initiated before the docking and before the momentum has ceased so that the final two or three feet of the approach end with the body either backing in or slipping in sideways. If the turn is initiated too far away from the docking the approach will simply run out of steam. Only practise will produce the effective 'back-in' or 'side-in'.

Jump no. 6 (from 9,000 ft minimum): *To introduce 'grip-switch' transitions and leg turns.*
You will exit first followed by your instructor, who will dock on you into a compressed accordian. He will then let go with his hand and you will swing around (still gripping with your hand) to form a two-man caterpillar. From this you will swing round again into a second compressed accordian. When your instructor has taken a grip of your leg, you will swing round yet again into another two-man caterpillar. Your instructor will then drop grips, you turn around and dock into a compressed accordian on the other side to that on which you docked originally and repeat the whole sequence the other way round.

Jump no. 7 (from 9,000 ft minimum): *To introduce 'vertical transitions'.*
Your instructor will follow you out, fly down and directly under you with

moderate speed, and then back over the top with about 3–6 ft vertical separation each time. You should feel the 'burble' of air as he passes underneath. It is now your turn to follow your instructor's example by flying both under then over him.

Jump no. 8 (from 10,000 ft minimum): *To introduce multiple formations and transitions.*
This jump is carried out with another student relative worker and your instructor. The latter will follow you both out of the aircraft. The two of you will set up opposite each other and level, a few feet apart. Your instructor will dock alongside one of you into a line. It is the turn of that student to move across, turn and dock alongside the other, again in a line. Complete one cycle of the exercise before varying it the second time around, with the person who is flying crossing in front of the person he has just left and S-turning into place on the third person. The secret of this exercise is to have two groups flying very close to one another. A variation of the jump is to dock into stairsteps instead of lines.

Jump no. 9 (from 10,000 ft minimum depending on numbers involved): *This exercise is for one, two or three student relative workers and an instructor.*
After exit you will form a no contact

'star', with one person carrying a baton of some sort. The idea is to pass the baton around the formation with the minimum of lateral movement. Everyone should concentrate on keeping the circle level and tight together more than on actually passing the baton.

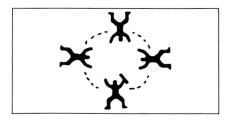

Jump no. 10 (from 10,000 ft minimum): *To introduce 'piece flying'.*
Both you and your instructor will exit simultaneously and form a stairstep with you at the rear. When formed your instructor will initiate a 180-degree turn towards you. You then grip-switch to your instructor's other leg and he will turn the stairstep in the opposite direction. You should concentrate on staying level with a tensionless grip and keeping your body parallel to your instructor's. After the second turn you will grip-shift into a caterpillar and your instructor will initiate a slow 360-degree barrel roll. These exercises may be done from lower altitudes, but you will not obtain so

Rules

Now for some of the golden rules of relative work:

1 Safety

This embodies every aspect of the jump. Checking that your equipment is serviceable and is not likely to open prematurely on exit. Keeping control of your speed in freefall and maintaining visual contact with those around you. Awareness of altitude is the responsibility of everyone in the group; make sure you break off at the correct altitude, turn 180° and track for your own piece of open sky for canopy deployment. It is important in early stages of relative work to establish for yourself a reputation of being someone who is safe in the sky—if the opposite occurs you will very soon find out that nobody wants to skydive with you.

2 Approach

If an approach starts going wrong or you find yourself moving in too fast, stop, and have another go. No one will ever criticise you for not having made it into the group, but, quite rightly, you can expect to be taken to task very firmly if your sloppy control or lack of experience has directly caused the breaking up of the group. The worst example of this is if you go low—do not allow

much working freefall time for your money if they are.

Floater

Before presenting some generally acceptable golden rules on relative work the term 'floater' needs explaining. A floater (or floaters) is that person who, before exit, moves into a position outside the fuselage of the aircraft and hangs on to grab-rails or handles to position himself to peel away into the slipstream as the exit starts. Floating, therefore, allows more

people to fly close to the initial group immediately after exit. The actual position and methods of peeling away from the aircraft will, of course, vary with aircraft type and this, once again, can only be practised on the ground beforehand. The danger of having too many floaters outside the aircraft before exit is the effect it will have on the aircraft's centre of gravity; therefore, it is important that the limitations imposed for that particular aircraft are strictly adhered to.

A round 'star' formation being built by the Royal Marines.

yourself to slide beneath the group. Again, no one will give you a hard time for the act of going low, but if you slide under the group, stealing their air and causing it to tumble, then quite rightly you can expect them to be upset about it.

3 Self-criticism

Be self-critical. Every relative work jump should have a comprehensive de-brief after it is over. Always admit your mistakes—there isn't a skydiver yet who hasn't made a mistake in his early days of relative work. Only then can you get the best from any jump and ensure that a similar situation doesn't happen again; there are always experienced people in a group who will help you solve your problems in a sympathetic way.

4 Planning

The success of any planned skydive is directly proportional to the amount of effort that has gone into it on the ground. A hastily conceived skydive with little or no dirt-diving will surely not go to plan. There is an old saying in flying: aviation in itself is not inherently dangerous; but to an even greater degree than the sea, it is terribly unforgiving of any carelessness, incapacity or neglect. In no aspect of sport parachuting does this apply more appropriately than to relative work.

Large formations

Once the basic skills of relative work have been mastered it will be perfectly natural to want to participate in large formations. The limitations here, of course, are the aircraft available and the constant maximum altitude of 12,000 ft (60-second delay). A number of aircraft flying in formation can readily increase the capacity of the load and potential for the formation. Formation flying does not present any real problems as the formations do not have to be wing-tip to wing-tip, but they do pose ones of organisation with different aircraft types climbing at different rates. This organisational problem is actually the one that is applicable by and large to every aspect of building big relative work formations. Ideally one man should be responsible for getting the team together, deciding the formation exit order and the all important pre-jump planning and dirt-dives. Exit order will primarily be decided by individual ability although the individual's weight may also present a problem, with the requirement for the heavier individual to be placed at the front of the load. (The heavier parachutist obviously has less flexibility in the variation of his rate of descent.) Teamwork is the key to building large formations successfully and this important factor must be considered throughout.

The first requirement is obviously a fast exit, and here again practice will produce the best situation. After exit a fast and stable base group must be formed. Make sure that you have plenty of experience in this group. If you do not, the slow build up of the group will adversely affect the rhythm of the entire skydive. The base group must ensure that it is falling fast and that it remains on a given heading. The base group now becomes the focal point of the skydive, with all the rest of the jumpers on the load having a fixed position or quadrant from which to make their approach. If the base group is rotating then of course there will be a tendency for the jumpers to take up the rotation in station and the remainder of the skydive will become a waste of time. Docking is also difficult if the group is in any way unstable; this instability could be caused by a poor docking or by bad flying from the members of the group already closed together. So the golden rule in the case of a group that is turning or falling unstably is to wait for it to settle on a heading before further docking.

The docking itself is another critical facet of the skydive, with essentially enough momentum to take the approaching skydiver straight to his position on arms or legs. As he docks there should be a natural inclination to pull in the legs, thus stopping any tendency to be flipped up and over into the group. As each jumper enters the formation his job is far from finished, for each must concentrate on 'flying' the formation to enable it to remain flat and stable. Basically each should try to fall level to the jumper opposite him by varying the amount of tucking of his arms and legs. As before, experience will be the school.

Finally the break up of the formation must take place at a higher altitude to allow the separation of all members of larger groups; it may even be necessary for this to be phased over 500 ft levels, with groups of jumpers breaking away at regular intervals. Once again, a comprehensive de-brief on the ground is important to correct any faults if the formation is to be attempted again.

Camera jumping

Relative work is visually exciting and so it is not surprising that all the best skydiving photographs feature this aspect of the sport. However, whilst being a natural extension of relative work, camera jumping also adds extra variables which may present pitfalls to the unwary. Two essential requirements for the ab initio camera jumper are obvious:

firstly, a basic competence at relative work, and secondly, a working knowledge of photography. I suggest a start is made taking still photos—cine or video are expensive ways of experimenting.

A motor-drive or auto-wind camera is a must because, as it is to be helmet-mounted (to allow for use of arms and hands in relative work), the film cannot be wound on manually in the normal way. For the same reason the shutter and winder must be electronically operated with cable and push button. The sighting provides the next problem, but there are two traditional solutions: first, the camera can be inverted when mounted, with the normal viewfinder being utilised, or secondly, a separate optical sight can be used which presupposes its careful alignment with the viewfinder before the jump. Another problem is that after exit from the aircraft, the camera settings cannot be altered. Focus is affected both by the 'f'-stop (the smaller the aperture, the greater the depth of focus), and the focal length of the lens (the wider the angle of the lens, the greater the depth of focus available). Therefore, a medium wide-angle lens (35 mm) is a good compromise when using a full frame 35 mm camera.

Professional assistance may be required when designing the camera mount, and the following should be taken into account:

1 Ensure there are two separate methods of securing the camera to the mount—the normal tripod bush on the camera base is not adequate on its own and nothing is worse than seeing a poorly mounted but expensive camera come loose and drop away in freefall.

2 The mount needs to position the camera as close to the helmet as possible for best balance.

3 Ensure that the design of the mount does not interfere with the working parts of the camera.

Having selected the equipment, the camera jump itself must now be considered. Choose a bright day and one with a few fluffy white cumulus clouds as background. Light, bright-coloured jumpsuits make for crisp pictures (black is a miserable colour for freefall photography), and try to jump well before or well after midday as the sun is then lower in the sky. Check the equipment's operation and settings carefully before emplaning. The cameraman's position should be considered from a potential photographic viewpoint. If the cameraman exits first he can obtain dramatic photographs of those following him out of the door; alternatively, following the group through the door provides another pleasing variation.

Experimentation during the actual skydive will influence the cameraman's positioning relative to the rest of the group. The budding cameraman should not be afraid to try new camera angles for the most novel or dramatic photographic result, but enormous care should be taken to ensure that photographic imagination and creativity does not influence altitude awareness or sound skydiving practice. Allow for extra briefing time and for extra height on the skydive itself if unusual photographs are to be taken, i.e. taking photographs of banners or canopy deployment. On the subject of canopy deployments the photographer who is just starting should be advised to steady his head with the helmet-mounted camera on board with his non-operative hand during canopy deployment; this will prevent any head-whip caused by a heavier than normal load on the helmet. There is often a temptation in the early days of camera jumping to be influenced by the enthusiasm of one's subjects or by the excitement of the potential of producing a dramatic skydiving photograph; these influences should not be allowed to colour sound judgment and care should be taken that photographic jumping does not take place in unsuitable conditions.

A fast exit from the Cessna 206.

Canopy relative work

The introduction of the ram-air canopy in the early 1970s brought about another challenging dimension to sport parachuting—canopy relative work (CRW). CRW is simply relative work after canopy deployment and may be described as contact formation canopy flying. As with other aspects of the sport it has its own particular appeal and devotees, but likewise it also has its own particular pitfalls and these

should be anticipated and the drills for countering them practised to ensure safe participation.

Equipment
Before becoming involved in CRW the equipment aspect should be considered. Certain types of equipment are potentially dangerous and should *not* be used in CRW. They are (a) Capewell canopy releases, (b) front mounted reserves other than those designed

specially for CRW, (c) cameras, (d) hard toggles, and (e) any type of pilot-chute controlled reefing system, including spider sliders (unless fitted with locking system). Other items of equipment are essential and should *always* be used in CRW; they are: (a) a sharp knife, positioned for easy access and operation, (b) gloves, (c) boots with ankle cover (a guard against line burn), (d) jump suit, (e) helmet (which does not restrict hearing), and (f) at least one working

Simon Ward's still and video camera helmet.

A CRW Tri-plane.

altimeter per group of four persons. Additionally it is useful to make certain canopy modifications, and they are as follows: (a) replace fly-away brakes with finger-trapped loops and knots, (b) fit soft toggles, (c) cross-port vent the canopy, (d) replace the V-shaped pilot-chute attachment with a single point attachment on the centre cell, and (e) replace centre 'B-line' cascade down to riser.

Simon Ward jumping with still and video cameras.

99

CRW can simply be added to the bottom end of a normal descent but in the early days it is vitally important to pre-plan the descent meticulously—take the aircraft to about 4,000 ft, clear and pull, and then concentrate only on CRW. The principal potential hazards are those of canopy collapses and entanglements and to this end no CRW should be initiated below 1,000 ft AGL—even this barely allows sufficient altitude to cut away and deploy the reserve parachute successfully.

As with freefall RW, your introduction to CRW should be with an instructor or tutor who is experienced at the game. At first you will be the high man and the 'target', and your instructor will be the 'aggressor' approaching you from below. The first two or three descents should be devoted to no contact formation flying to assimilate the behaviour of the two canopies relative to one another. Once both canopies are flying and you have located each other, you must first manoeuvre into the same general airspace. At this stage radical loss of altitude may be achieved by judicious use of the front risers. As target you should position yourself with your instructor off to one side, low, and on the same heading inside his radius of turn. Having turned the canopy to about half brake you should initiate

a very slow turn towards your instructor; this is the extent of setting yourself up as the target.

You should now listen out for instructions from your instructor. If he has a faster rate of descent and goes too low he might ask you to carry out a quick stall and recover to rectify the situation. If he has a slower rate of descent, he might ask you to let up your brakes to enable you to move up relative to him. Meanwhile your instructor will be making gentle corrections as he moves close to you, flying no contact initially, then eventually closing to make a hook-up. The hook-up will be effected by your instructor's canopy coming into contact with you behind your knees and you should then take a hold of the leading edge of the upper surface of his canopy. As each hand takes a grip the toggle may be released; if undue oscillations are set up your instructor should let go and start again. If you are not positioned in the centre of his canopy a two-handed grip can move hand to hand along the leading edge to the centre of the canopy. You can now hook your feet into the sides of the 'channel' so that the leading edge is across your ankles. You can then stand up and take the toggles, and in so doing gain control of both canopies which you can steer in the normal way. With experience a CRW hook-

up can be flown down to the landing.

Safety rules
There are a number of basic safety rules in CRW and if these are disregarded accidents can be anticipated.

1 Before attempting CRW a parachutist should have at least 100 jumps on a ram-air canopy, and should thoroughly understand that canopy's characteristics, i.e. can a smooth, gentle, accurate approach be made and a smooth stall recovery executed?

2 Dock softly, don't rush and think you can sort it out once you are in! You may not be able to. If your approach is fast, turn off and start again.

3 Hit with the centre cell; it is a simple matter to pass the leading edge from hand to hand until you arrive at the centre cell, but it wastes time and tends to start oscillation.

4 Take a grip on the leading edge—grabbing any other part of the canopy may cause it to collapse.

5 Dock from directly astern, as docking at even a slight angle will initiate oscillation.

6 Do not go in front of the stack—your canopy wash may

cause a collapse. If you find yourself in front execute a front riser turn away, but be aware of other canopies approaching to dock.

7 If, when approaching to dock, the parachutist you are aiming at disappears above your canopy, execute a front riser turn away, attempting to back up on brakes; or toggle turn will give you lift into or in front of the stack. In either case you will not be too popular with the other parachutists.

8 No CRW below 1,000 ft (mandatory); if you tend to be aggressive do not carry out CRW below 1,500 ft.

9 Once in the stack, constantly check your own canopy. Should end-cell closure occur, re-inflate immediately. Most collapses start with end-cell closures. Unless you intend to land formations, break off above 1,000 ft (beware of pilot-chutes).

10 No transitions in sequential CRW below 2,000 ft.

11 Make sure you communicate and that all members of the stack know what is happening.

The dangers of CRW become amplified and very evident when either a canopy collapse occurs or when parachutists become entangled. In either situation it is essential to stay calm and the following are given as actions for these situations:

Canopy collapse actions
A collapse involves two parachutists and in all cases the bottom man must make the decision as to whether he can re-inflate or would prefer to be dropped. A collapse only becomes hazardous when there are other canopies close by, either in the stack or approaching to dock. If there is any sort of problem in the stack on your approach to dock, turn off and steer clear until the problem is sorted out.

1 If you are holding a canopy which collapses, (a) do not drop it, the parachutist may fall into another canopy below. (b) Remember it is the low man who makes the decision, so listen for his instructions. (c) If the low man asks to be dropped, do so immediately. (d) If you are told to hold on, then do so.

2 If your canopy collapses, (a) stay calm and try to pump it out; the stroke is from full brakes up to quarter brakes and then back down again with a smooth and gentle pump. Often collapses can be sorted out this way. (b) If your canopy will not re-inflate, first check below. If there are canopies in the stack below inform the parachutist immediately beneath you of your problem and ensure he has control of his own canopy before dropping him. Regardless of the amount of canopies below, they should move away as a group, and should not approach the stack again until the collapse has been sorted out. (c) Once clear below, check your height, apply full brakes and inform the parachutist above to drop you. However bad your collapse, providing you are on full brakes you will not drop further than 30 ft, but you must be on full brakes, since trying to re-inflate a collapse in a full drive configuration is risking a malfunction. (d) Once you are back in full control carry out all-round observation.

Entanglement drills
Most entanglements occur when a collapsed canopy is dropped without warning, thereby allowing the collapse to fall into the canopy below, so remember, 'don't let go'. If you have a pilot-chute around you, take your knife and cut the bridle-line. If you have any other type of entanglement, you have a major problem and may have to cut away, but first check your height. Then check your problem, because if the canopy is still inflated you should be able to untangle yourself, ensuring that there is no slack line around the reserve handle or the cut-away pad. Before you decide to cut away ensure that you are not

attached by any other part of your body or equipment, and make sure you are clear below. Also ensure that the other parachutists are aware of your intentions.

These are the ground rules and advice for CRW. Take it steady, step by step, with an experienced tutor and CRW will provide you with enormous fun and satisfaction.

The bottom man docking to make it a '7-stack'.

17. Competitive parachuting

In 1951, five nations met in Yugoslavia for a parachuting competition which was, in essence, the first world championships, but it was not until the second world championships were held at St Yan in France in 1954 that the Fédération Aéronautique Internationale recognised parachuting as a sport and its International Parachuting Committee (CIP) became responsible for its organisation and administration. Since then world parachuting championships have been held in accordance with the provisions of chapter 5 (Parachuting) of the FAI's Sporting Code as follows: 1956—Tushino, Russia; 1958—Bratislavia, Czechoslovakia; 1960—Sofia, Bulgaria; 1962—Orange, USA; 1964—Leutkirch, West Germany; 1966—Leipzig, East Germany; 1968—Graz, Austria; 1970—Bled, Yugoslavia; 1972—Talequah, USA; 1974—Szolnok, Hungary; 1975—Warendorf, West Germany (RW); 1976—Guidonia, Italy (Classic events); 1977—Gatton, Australia (RW); 1978—Zagreb, Yugoslavia (Classic); 1979—Chateauroux, France (RW); 1980—Kazanlak, Bulgaria (Classic); 1981—Zephyr-hills, USA (RW); 1982—Lucenec, Czeckoslovakia (Classic); 1983—Sun City, South Africa (RW); 1984—Vichy, France (Classic); and 1985—Malilosinj, Yugoslavia (RW).

World championships in sport parachuting were originally centred around the style and accuracy events—these have now become known as the 'Classic Events'. In 1975 the first world championships in relative work took place at Warendorf in West Germany and have featured thereafter every other year. In early 1985 the CIP decided that CRW and Para-Ski should also become world championship events.

Competing for one's nation in world parachute championships can obviously only be for the select and talented few; although of those chosen many have attained this goal through sheer dedication and hard work. This does not mean that competition is for the exclusive few; it can be enjoyed at all levels and this section is aimed at explaining competitive parachuting so that the maximum enjoyment from participating can be achieved. Probably most parachutists do not have the whole-hearted patience, dedication and self-discipline that is required of a top line competition jumper. You cannot expect to represent your country or to achieve top honours without a good deal of frustration and single-minded determination, but nevertheless the satisfaction of success, no matter how small, may well be ample reward. Although parachute competitions can take many

different forms (and here the not so expert parachutist can enjoy the invention and participation in novel types of competition), the only types of event that are currently used in world competition are the five events already mentioned: style, accuracy, relative work, CRW and para-ski.

Style is the individual ability to perform fast, precise manoeuvres in freefall. Accuracy may be an individual or team event where the aim is to land as close as possible to a pre-designated target on the ground. Relative work has two competitive events and these are the eight-man team and the four-man team sequential events. The requirement in each of these is to perform the maximum number of formations in a sequence in so many seconds of freefall working time. In canopy relative work there are three simple events: first is the speed stack event which is based on the ability to build an eight-man canopy stack as fast as possible; then there is the four-way rotation event where a number of four-man canopy stacks are built in a given period; and finally there is the four-man sequential event where a number of different formations are made in a given time period. Lastly, in para-ski there is a combination of accuracy and skiing.

It now remains to describe these events in more detail and to provide a few coaching tips to help you in your early days of competition. It is not possible to go into great detail as the specific rules tend to be updated by CIP on an annual basis, but individual national associations should have copies of the detailed current rules available. The reading and interpretation of these rules are a very important part of the preparation for any competition, and will often result in a welcome re-jump or a reversal of a judge's decision. Finally, do not forget to read the important competitive sections in chapter 5 of the *FAI Sporting Code*.

Style

Style jumps are made from 2,000 metres (6,600 ft). This allows approximately 27 seconds to exit the aircraft, build up to terminal velocity, align with the heading arrow on the ground and perform the six manoeuvres of the style series, before opening the canopy at 2,000 ft. The basic rules of style are straightforward. Competitors will normally each perform four jumps (which form the four rounds of the event) and they will each perform the same series in any one round. The full style series is:

Group 1 (left series)—left turn, right turn, backloop, left turn, right turn, backloop.

Group 2 (right series)—right turn, left turn, backloop, right turn, left turn, backloop.

Group 3 (left cross series)—left turn, right turn, backloop, right turn, left turn, backloop.

Group 4 (right cross series)—right turn, left turn, backloop, left turn, right turn, backloop.

The judging area will be readily visible from the air and competitors will use this as a reference point on which to hold a heading during their performance. As accuracy plays no part in style the parachutist will be given an exit command from the ground by the judges, which will be chosen for ease of viewing each jumper's performance using a video system. After exit from the aircraft terminal velocity should be achieved before the competitor starts the series to avoid the sloppiness of sub-terminal manoeuvre. During this build-up to terminal velocity the competitor should line up precisely with the judging area and reduce his own surface area dramatically before spinning into the first turn. Style is judged on two features: speed and precision. Each manoeuvre must be carried out as fast as possible with complete precision so that each turn and loop is completed with the jumper on heading with the judge. Penalty points are deducted for

under-shooting and over-shooting turns (the exact number of penalty points varies with the degree of over-shoot and under-shoot), rolling off loops or failing to complete them on heading and for carrying out manoeuvres with the body inclined off a vertical axis. Loss of all points will occur if the parachutist performs the wrong series, omits any manoeuvre from the correct series, or performs additional manoeuvres to those prescribed for that particular series.

When you take up style jumping you should concentrate initially on precision (or turning a 'clean' series), rather than on speed. Once you can turn a well co-ordinated clean series you can then start to cut down on the time. In theory it has been calculated by models in wind tunnels that the minimum time for each manoeuvre is between 8 and 9 tenths of a second, which gives a total theoretical time of 4.8 to 5.4 seconds for a series. But of course this assumes perfect performance and no time gap between each manoeuvre. There is a subconscious tendency when starting style to practise one particular series and the mistake of doing this is obvious, so write up each successive style jump in your log book showing its type and time, together with relevant criticisms. Time spent practising on the ground in a suspended harness is invaluable and will do much to assist your co-ordination. If you can have a colleague observing you either from the ground with binoculars (or better still video) or in freefall, so much the better as you are more likely to learn from someone else's critique than from your own.

Accuracy

Accuracy jumps are made from 600–1,000 metres (2,200 to 3,200 ft) depending on local rules. Where there is a jump altitude of 3,000 ft the competitor has the flexibility of opening between 0 and 10 seconds after exit, which means that he can alter his length of time under the canopy to adjust the spot if necessary. The number of accuracy jumps in a competition may vary, but 10 has become a usual figure which means that a good accuracy jumper must also be consistent. The 'target area' is a circular pit of fine pea-gravel at least 30 metres in diameter. The 'dead centre' (DC) of the target area is marked with an orange fluorescent disc which is 5 centimetres in diameter. The inside ends of the four arms of the target cross are 5 metres. This allows a circle of 10 metres in diameter of clear pea-gravel with the disc in the centre. Distance of landing is measured to the nearest centimetre from the edge of the disc and

hitting the disc itself scores 0·00 for the competitor. Every centimetre out scores 0·01 points to a maximum of 5 metres, making the maximum score 5 points. The winner is, therefore, the competitor who scores the lowest total number of points. The distance from the DC is measured to the first point of bodily contact; for instance, if the disc is hit with the right foot but the trailing foot touches down first then it is to the left foot that measurement is taken. In national and international competition you can expect that an electronic scoring pad of some 40 centimetres in diameter will be used for accurately measuring the top contenders.

Ram-air canopy technique
The typical ram-air canopy technique is now described, bearing in mind that the final approach to the DC disc is made into wind. In planning the whole flight pattern it is worth considering the final approach first. Ideally it should be initiated from about 100 metres (or 400 ft). If the surface wind is on the accuracy limit of 7 metres per second, the final approach should be made from about 25 metres downwind of the disc, adding 25 metres for each metre per second that the surface wind speed decreases. These distances also give an approximation as to the distance you by-pass the target on

the downwind leg of the flight pattern at 1,000 ft. Having flown the first half of the canopy descent position yourself abeam the target at 1,000 ft AGL facing downwind and ensure that you are now on half brakes. Remaining on half brakes continue downwind, before turning onto the base leg and ultimately into wind onto final approach at the 400 ft AGL 'attack' point. From this attack point to the ground you should not take your eyes off the disc for an instant, concentrating on gently increasing or decreasing the brakes, depending on whether you are going to over-shoot or under-shoot the disc. It is also important that you are precisely on the windline at the attack point otherwise you will have another variable to correct during these last critical 20 seconds of the descent.

In the early stages of accuracy jumping you should ensure your canopy handling is gentle in the extreme. The experienced ram-air accuracy jumper will make a high approach onto the disc in very deep brakes; thus his movement over the ground is minimal but, of course, the dangers of inadvertently stalling the canopy are obvious. Canopy stability during this part of the approach is vital. It may also help to raise your goggles to avoid optical distortion and to undo your chest strap to allow more freedom of

A simple 9-way formation.

movement. Perfect control of the canopy must be maintained to the second of touch down, so any temptation to let go of the toggles must be resisted. Ideally, one toe or heel should strike first, with the other tucked up out of the way. The final reach for the disc is the key to hitting it consistently so avoid the tendency to use the same foot on every jump—reach with the most convenient foot. Any violent body movement in the harness will upset canopy trim, therefore restrict your

106

final reach if necessary to the final second or two and only when it is absolutely essential. In the early days watching the experts will be most helpful to you, as will having constructive critiques on your own performance.

Re-jumps
Under certain conditions re-jumps may be awarded and to explain these in detail it is simply easiest to quote direct from chapter 5 of the Sporting Code:

'1 Any malfunction of the main parachute canopy which creates a control problem for the parachutist may merit a re-jump. In this case the parachutist must indicate immediately that he has such a problem by signalling with his arms or legs outstretched, or other suitable signal, through most of the descent and must make no attempt to land in the target area.

2 Inspection of the equipment and/or verification by an official

All freefall and CRW events are judged using video.

Eyes on the disc, right toe reaching for the disc.

appointed by the Chief Judge or Event Judge immediately after the competitor has landed must indicate that the jumper did suffer a malfunction that was not created by the jumper himself.

3 A control problem is interpreted to mean that a condition in the deployment of the parachute exists such that it is virtually impossible to safely attempt a precision target approach, or that the main canopy configuration is such as to prevent the competitor from demonstrating his skill.

4 If there is a sudden change in ground wind direction of more than 90° when the wind speed is more than 3 metres per second during the final approach of a competitor he/she will be granted a re-jump. The judges at the target shall decide if the competitor was on final approach and their decision is no grounds for a protest. This rule shall only be used when the wind direction is automatically recorded.

5 If, during the accuracy events, two or more competitors approach and/or land on the target simultaneously and in the process interfere with each other the judges at the target, and including the event judge, may authorise a re-jump for one, or both or neither. Other judges may give evidence or information if relevant, but will not take part in the final vote. If such an interference occurs between members of the same team during team accuracy jumps, no re-jump will be granted.

6 If a competitor accidentally strikes a judge before reaching the ground, he must be awarded a re-jump.

7 If an AMD (automatic measuring device) is found to be defective or not electronically reset and the first point of contact has been on it, the competitor shall make a re-jump. If a competitor lands outside an

uncentred automatic measuring device he shall make a re-jump.

8 Competitors who land after an interruption shall not be measured and must execute a re-jump.'

Team accuracy event

In the team accuracy event the team will consist of four members and the jumps shall be made from an altitude of 1,000 metres. The team must jump from the same aircraft, during one passage of the aircraft over the target. If meteorological conditions do not allow jumping from 1,000 metres, the altitude may be lowered to 800 metres for a whole round. A team may jump with less than four members. The missing team member shall be awarded the maximum score for the jump. To avoid individual members conflicting with each other during the final approach, the openings should be stacked up to avoid all landings in the pit simultaneously. The method of doing this is simple: the first man exits the aircraft and opens on about 8 seconds; each successive team member exits in turn with an approximate two-second gap between each. They then deploy their parachutes as they see the canopy of the low man start to deploy. This will give openings on about 8 seconds for the first man, 6 for the second, 4 for the third, and 2 seconds for the last

man to leave the aircraft.

It is important that the weight of each jumper is considered; it may be that a heavy man out last may upset the stack or, conversely, it may be that a light man out last will be affected by winds above 2,500 ft (but these may fail to affect those in the team whose canopies are open below this height). The final point to remember about team jumping is to get out of the way the moment you land in order that your team-mates may have a clear run and so that the judges have an unobstructed view. You can see, therefore, that team jumping will need extra planning before the event even though most of the problems will have been sorted out during practice.

Relative work

The eight- and four-man sequential RW events are proper team events for if one man fails to do his job properly the team could easily score zero points. The following, quoted verbatim from chapter 5 of the Sporting Code, describes the event: 'Definition of four-man/eight-man tests:

1 Each round will consist of a sequence of scoring formations shown in the competition rules. The transition between each scoring formation will be either by way of a

Above Examples of 4-man random formations: (a) star, (b) Danish tee, (c) zig-zag, (d) box.

Below Examples of 8-man random formations: (a) zipper, (b) donut, (c) star.

(a) (b) (c) (d)

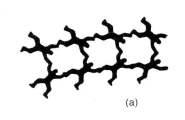  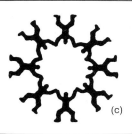

(a) (b) (c)

specified 'inter' as shown in the competition rules or by way of a 'free transition' with complete separation between all jumpers. A draw will determine the sequence to be performed in each round of the event. On the correct completion of each sequence it should be repeated until the expiry of the alotted working time.

2 Where flying groups are shown as 'inters' they must remain intact as a group from the break of the previous formation until the correct completion of the next formation in the sequence. Should a sub-group or formation separate from a completed configuration in a

manner other than prescribed, they must re-form the last correctly completed configuration. A correctly completed configuration is defined as a formation which is recorded correct by the majority of the judges.'

The four-man event will be from 2,750 metres (9,000 ft) with a working time of 35 seconds. The eight-man event will be from 3,500 metres (11,500 ft) with a working time of 50 seconds.

The draw of the sequences will be supervised by the Chief Judge and teams will be given not less than 2 hours knowledge of the results of the draw before the competition

starts. All the 'blocks' (numbered) and the 'formations' (alphabetically marked) shown in the competition rules will be placed separately in a single container. Individual consecutive draws from the container will determine the sequence to be jumped in each round. Each round will be drawn so as to consist of 5 or 6 scoring formations, whichever number is reached first. Should the draw determine that two identical formations are repeated consecutively, one of the two formations will be removed from the sequence or, if two blocks are drawn, they will be linked by the identical formation to a three-formation block. If two formations are drawn consecutively between which only one team member changes position, the second formation or block will be re-drawn at the discretion of the Chief Judge. In a sequence drawn each block or formation will be drawn once only.

There is no limitation on the exit procedure other than that imposed by the Chief Pilot for aircraft safety reasons. The exit point will be controlled by a radio command from the ground relayed from the pilot to the team in the aircraft. It will consist of the commands 'run-in', 'stand-by' then 'exit'.

The performance requirement is somewhat complicated but here again it is best to quote from the official words in chapter 5:

'**1** All configurations shall consist of jumpers linked by grips. A grip for scoring purposes shall consist of a hand-hold on an arm or leg as required by the illustrations in the competition rules.

2 Each formation, sub-groups and intermediate requirements must be performed in accordance with the illustrations in the appropriate competition rules. Mirror images of all completed blocks and/or random formations are acceptable. Formations need not be perfectly symmetrical.

3 When a turn is indicated a sub-group must continue turning in the direction of the arrow until it is possible for the sub-groups to link together to complete the next designated formation. The degree of turn as shown in the competition rules indicates the approximate degree of turn required to show the intent of the transition manoeuvre. The approximate degree of turn required shows that the indicated sub-groups must present that amount of its circumference to the other sub-group.

4 When separation is indicated it must be performed in such a manner that there is no physical contact between sub-groups or individual jumpers.

5 To score points it is a requirement that all formations, sub-groups, intermediate requirements and various configurations are executed in such a manner that will demonstrate to the judges on the ground that the required performance has been achieved.

6 A malfunction is no grounds for a re-jump.'

The scoring system is simple. Each team shall score one point per formation completed correctly. Points may only be scored within the working time. Omission of a formation, or incorrect formation, or an incorrect inter prior to a formation will stop the scoring for that formation and the next two correctly completed formations according to the prescribed sequence. Scoring will resume with the completion of three correctly completed consecutive formations following the stop in scoring. Scoring may also continue with the correct completion of the omitted formation, or incorrect formation, or formation prior to the incorrect inter and continuation of the prescribed sequence. The winner in both events is the team that accumulates the highest total number of points during the competition.

Success in relative work competition comes about through accomplished skill of basic relative work coupled with a determined team spirit which strives for perfection through constant practice and self-criticism. As video is the primary judging facility for relative work it is important that it is used as much as possible during training for this competition. It will enable teams to see what the judges see from the ground, and whether their performance is executed in accordance with the rules. The success of the relative work events over the years has evolved because of the team element and because it is a freefall event which is based on what most skydivers are doing at weekends anyway. Therefore, even if one is not a dedicated competitor in this

A 4-way event block sequence—arrowhead to diamond.

An 8-way event block sequence—snow flake to in-out.

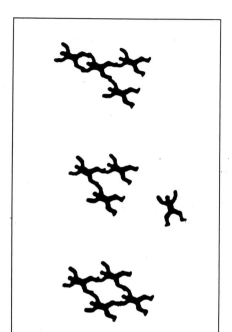

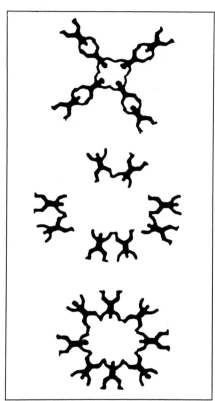

event enormous enjoyment can be achieved by simply trying out some of the sequences as shown in the diagrams. As in all competition, the principal criteria are determined aggression to win coupled with practised expertise.

Canopy Relative Work

Before we can look at CRW competition it is worth having a look at some definitions. In CRW teams perform a canopy formation or a sequence of canopy formations during the descent under the open canopy. To qualify as a legal formation the following requirements must be met:

(a) All parachutists are connected by legal grips; and

(b) all parachutes are fully open and under control.

A canopy with more than two collapsed end cells will not be accepted as an open canopy. Swinging canopies do not necessarily show lack of control.

A legal grip may be defined as at least one secure point of contact between a jumper and the canopy, lines, risers, harness, body or clothing of another jumper. In a 'stack' configuration the shoulders of the upper jumper must be above the top skin of the lower canopy and the grip must be on the centre cell or on a line adjacent to the centre cell. In a 'plane' configuration the head of the upper jumper must be below the bottom skin of the lower canopy and the grip must be on a line adjacent to the centre cell or on the risers, harness, clothing or body of the lower jumper. In a 'stairstep' configuration the grip must be on an end cell or a line adjacent to the end cell and the top jumper's body must be mostly outside the line that is next to the end line. If a diagram shows a jumper on top of and in contact with both canopies, the rule for stairstep grips applies. The location of a grip must be as indicated in the diagrams of the current competition rules. The judges may infer the existence or non-existence of a legal grip from the behaviour of the formation if the grip itself cannot be directly viewed and video back-up does not solve

Examples of 4-way random formations: (a) inverted tee, (b) stack plane, (c) stacked stairsteps.

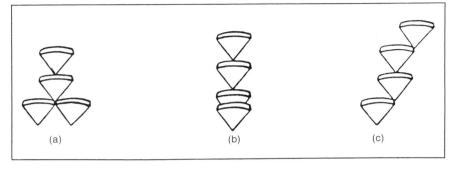

(a)   (b)   (c)

the problem. In case of uncertainty on the part of a majority of the judges, a re-jump shall be granted.

A sequence may be described as formation changes during a jump as directed by the competition rules. An intermediate requirement is a step between two formations. Complete separation of all team members or two or more jumpers flying together as one or more pre-determined groups. And finally working time starts when the first team member leaves the aircraft after the stand-by or exit command has been given. For the purpose of this rule, cameramen, judges or observers approved to jump with the team shall be deemed as team members.

CRW events

There are three different events in CRW:

1 The eight-way event is from 5,000 ft with a working time of 100 seconds. Each round consists of a single plane/stack formation which must be held for at least 10 seconds. The holding time may run over the working time.

2 The four-way rotation event is from 7,200 ft with a working time of 180 seconds. Each round consists of successive four-way plane/stack formations being made by rotations. Rotations must be made by the top competitor in the formation

dropping grips, flying to the bottom of the formation and again completing a four-canopy formation. If the top competitor drops grips before the formation is complete, the formation will be considered to have been incorrectly completed.

3 The four-way sequential event is from 8,200 ft with a working time of 240 seconds. Each round consists of a sequence of formations as described in the competition rules. On completion of each sequence it can be repeated until the working time has elapsed. The draw for the sequences will be supervised by the Chief Judge and teams will be given not less than two hours knowledge of the results of the draw before the competition starts.

In CRW malfunctions will be grounds for re-jumps. Remaining team members shall not engage in CRW during the rest of the descent. If CRW takes place, the team shall

be scored in the normal manner, even though they have an incomplete team. The judges will exercise common sense if a late exit member has a malfunction and the front exit members are already engaged in CRW. A malfunction that does not occur on deployment will not automatically constitute a re-jump for the team.

The scoring in each event is as follows:

1 Eight-way speed event. One point is scored for each legally connected competitor, provided the grips are held for 10 seconds. The holding time may run over the working time. Docking times, break-up time and re-building time are recorded. If two or more canopies dock simultaneously each shall be awarded the same docking time. Time shall be recorded to the nearest hundredth of a second. The value of each jump is the time taken to build an eight-stack/plane.

A 4-way set sequence.

2 Four-way rotation event. One point is scored for every correctly completed four-way formation inside the working time on each jump.

3 Four-way sequential event. One point is scored for each completed formation as shown in the diagrams of the competition rules. Points may only be scored within the working time.

Of course the team in each event who scores the highest number of points over the total number of rounds is the winner.

The rotation event is probably the best training for all of the three CRW events. It is the perfect example of teamwork and communication combined with CRW skills. Each team member in the four-man plane (quadraplane) has different jobs to do on succession and only constant practice will achieve consistent results. For instance, when number four has made his initial docking number three must immediately shout 'On!' and at that instant number one kicks out of the riser bars and applies sufficient brakes to stop a surge forward and to rise up in front of the stack, whereupon number two takes control. Number one is now faced with the job of flying back over and behind the stack through its inherent burble before re-docking on the bottom. It is a

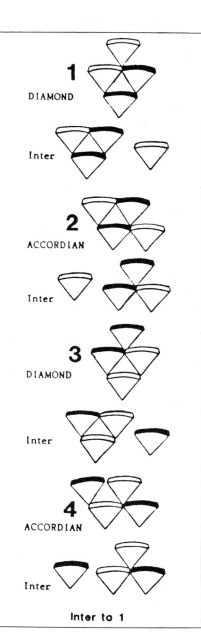

good event because each team member is working hard all the time to carry out successfully his part of the sequence.

CRW has only just received the status of being a world championship event and it is obviously an event with a stimulating future because CRW, being essentially visual, will probably attract sponsorship in a way that competitive events have failed to do in the past. We can, therefore, expect to see some very exciting world championships in CRW in the future.

Para-Ski

In Para-Ski parachutists compete in both accuracy and giant-slalom ski racing. The rules for the accuracy part of Para-Ski have already been described and the rules for the giant slalom are as laid down in the championship rules, being outside the scope of this book. Para-Ski, therefore, combines two totally separate sporting disciplines and attracts its own particular devotees.

Judging

Any sport parachute competition will be judged by a panel of judges organised by the Chief Judge assisted by Event Judges as required. A judge need not necessarily be a parachutist at all—there are numerous non-

stating the particular rule or rules about which the protest is being made. Finally it is worth making the point that if competitors receive fair and accurate judgment at national level, they will be better prepared for competing at world level.

Training
There is no doubt that, to achieve honours in sport parachuting competition, there is no substitute for making literally hundreds of parachute jumps in practice. This in itself will produce a reasonable standard of fitness, but couple the parachute training with running, circuit training and, maybe, the odd game of squash, and the benefits will be enormous; co-ordination will be improved while both physical and mental well-being will do much to counteract competition tension on the day.

The right attitude for competitive success is a combination of calm relaxation and total concentration. In the early days this attitude will have to be developed by observing successful adversaries, and learning from their competitive behaviour is definitely beneficial as is ignoring the poor example of those who throw tantrums or who blame anyone other than themselves after a poor performance. This competitive behaviour is called sportsmanship—good or bad.

jumping wives and girlfriends of sport parachutists who have become accomplished judges. Judges are highly qualified, initially at national level, and subsequently as FAI international judges in accordance with standards laid down in chapter 5 of the Sporting Code and reviewed regularly by CIP. Every judge must keep a log book and a record of his judging and must successfully judge a minimum number of competitions annually to keep his qualification valid. Every competition will be preceded by a briefing by the Chief Judge and, as

total understanding of the rules is vital to competitive success, this is the competitors' final opportunity for clarification of any aspect of the rules.

Judges have a thankless task to perform, even though they have the benefit of video and electronic measuring systems. So a good competitor will respect their decisions, even if these are sometimes disappointing for him personally. While scores may not be protested, at national and international level it is possible to protest to the competition jury

18. Display parachuting

Display parachuting is the presentation of the sport to the general public who will judge it by what they see. All display parachutists, and particularly jumpmasters and instructors, who accept the responsibility for giving displays must take into account the risks and possible consequences of displays which misfire. Sound judgment should never be influenced by the desire not to disappoint the crowd and the organisers. Injuries sustained in public and parachutists who land outside the area have an adverse affect on responsible opinion, since they usually result from incompetence or jumping in unsuitable conditions. Display parachuting, therefore, calls for the

A display landing at the start of a World Championships.

highest standards of planning, co-ordination, experience, mutual confidence, safety-consciousness and parachuting skills. For these reasons parachutists who cannot be relied upon to do what is expected of them should not be permitted to take part in displays.

It is, of course, important that each team must have a nominated team leader. In Britain the qualifications for that have been laid down in the *BPA Operations Manual*:

'All display teams must have a team leader who is a BPA approved instructor, has made at least 300 jumps and has made at least 30 display jumps or is an FAI D Certificate parachutist, who has made at least 300 jumps, has made at least 30 display jumps and has passed an examination, administered by a National Coach and Safety Officer, on display procedures and pilot and aircraft requirements. The team leader is responsible for the safe conduct of all parachuting and flying operations carried out by that team, in accordance with the *BPA Operations Manual*. The BPA and CAA should be notified in writing not less than 7 days in advance of any intended change of team leader.'

Once the team leader has been nominated the team itself must now be registered with the BPA and then an application made to the Civil Aviation Authority for an annual Display Permission. The registration with the BPA is straightforward and the form at Appendix E of the *BPA Operations Manual* is self-explanatory. It should be completed and forwarded to the BPA office who will in turn send the team a BPA Display Team Certificate and registration number. Once the BPA have issued the display team with its Certificate and registered display team number the form at Appendix F of the *BPA Operations Manual* can now be completed and sent to the Civil Aviation Authority (whose address is on the bottom of the form) who will then issue the necessary Display Team Permission. It should be noted that the CAA require at least 28 days from the date of receipt of a completed application to issue the necessary permission, so ensure that you do not leave this procedure until the last minute.

Order of events

The display can be examined by chronological order of events, bearing in mind that its planning will undoubtedly be reflected in the final result. Having received the initial enquiry from the show organiser you should arrange to meet him on the actual site for the display about six weeks before the event. You should arm yourself with a one-inch to one-mile map of the area, the northern or southern aeronautical chart ICAO 1:500, 1,000, available from your local flying club, together with paper and pencil. The show organisers should be asked to produce a six-inch to one-mile map of the showground and its surrounding areas and, if there is any difficulty over this, advise them to approach the local borough surveyor for a photostat copy. The show organisers should also be asked to produce written permission from the owners of the land for the parachute display to take place and approval from the local police (both these are CAA requirements).

The organiser may well have some preconceived ideas about the capabilities of your team and you should immediately point out your limitations and how wind and cloud may affect your display on the day. Overshoot areas are very important as they can allow a certain margin of error; they should be considered in the light of the prevailing wind, but of course even this may change on the day and the DZ should be examined bearing this in mind. The *BPA Operations Manual*, Section 13, Display Parachuting, Paragraph 3 lays down the qualifications for team members and at this stage these are worth quoting in full:
'(a) Parachutists holding FAI D Certificates may give displays using

DZs of not less than 75 yards in diameter, which are free from major hazards and providing not more than 10% of this area is not taken up with minor hazards. In all such cases, however, adequate

The pre-display 'dirt dive'.

overshoot areas must exist on all sides.
(b) FAI C Certificate holders may give displays providing that:
1 They have made at least 100 sport parachute descents.
2 The DZ is at least 150 yards in diameter.

3 They are approved for such displays by their CCIs.
4 The aircraft is carrying a jumpmaster who is a BPA instructor.
5 There are adequate overshoot areas on at least 3 sides of the DZ.'
The most difficult part of your planning visit to the display drop

zone is to imagine how it will look on the day with car parks, marquees and side shows filling your carefully chosen overshoot areas to capacity. This problem should be fully discussed with the show organiser and all these

hazards should be marked accurately on the six-inch to one-mile plan of the show ground. You can then check the aeronautical chart to see if the DZ lies in controlled airspace or under an airway, and possibly tell the

organiser of any problem that there might be in this respect. Sometimes it is very difficult to refuse an enthusiastic show organiser his display for a perfectly valid reason which he may not fully understand, but if you have the slightest doubt

A 5-way 'star' formation.

A British 4-man team (the R.A.F.) in a 'diamond'.

about its feasibility you should take this course of action.

Having agreed to undertake the display, however, you can now discuss the exact details of the event with the organisers. The financial side of it should be tied up with a written agreement based on aircraft flying time at '£X per hour', cost per individual parachutist and a cancellation fee in case of bad weather. It is best to give a quote to the organiser which will not be exceeded, and it should be pointed out that in addition to the cancellation fee there could be some aircraft positioning and landing fees to pay for. At the mention of cancellation fees some organisers will visibly show their disapproval but you should point out that freefall displays are always a good crowd draw and that the crowd will normally have paid their gate money well before the display is called unless it is a really terrible day for the weather.

You can then discuss the timings for the display and here it is helpful to point out that the weather tends to be best for parachuting later in the day and, of course, the later the display is scheduled the longer the crowd is kept in the show ground. If you are doing more than one display on the same day you should allow plenty of time for repacking and travelling to the mounting airfield. Another useful point worth mentioning to the organiser is that having picked the time for the display he should try to stick to it; if the aircraft arrives overhead on time with horses and jumps still in the arena it is the organisers who will have to pay for the extra flying time involved while they clear the drop zone.

Medical cover should normally present no problem, but a medical pack is a useful part of your own DZ equipment. Crowd control is another subject for discussion as quite often it is non-existent at smaller shows and can provide the harrassed jumper with another hazard. You should also mention your DZ control and commentary arrangements; most organisers are more than pleased for you to provide your own commentator but

you should check the latter can see all that is happening from where the microphone is located. As part of this discussion you can mention any communication systems you are operating between the drop zone and the aircraft and how they can help in the smooth running of the show.

The next part of your display preparation concerns the flying side. Ideally you should use the same aircraft and pilot for all your displays so that you can build up a smooth operating system which will hep you to achieve the best results with the minimum of fuss. When you engage a pilot for the first time ensure he is qualified to drop parachutists and that the aircraft is similarly cleared for parachuting with the necessary authorisation within its Certificate of Airworthiness. The airfield from which you mount the display may not be the aircraft's base and therefore you should check that the pilot has fuel and hangarage arranged if necessary. Remember that landing and hangarage fees have to be considered in your original estimate as most airfields charge them.

The nearest meteorological office will probably be at the mounting airfield but you should check on this and have its phone number readily available. The difference in altitude between the drop zone and

the mounting airfield should be ascertained from the map so that altimeters can be adjusted to read the correct altitude above the drop zone. Finally, in company with the organiser, a visit to the local police may be necessary if they are not entirely happy about your display. This visit will hopefully ensure their co-operation at an event where the safety of the general public is one of their primary concerns.

Having visited the show organiser ensure that you have with you the written permission of the land owner, the written approval of the local police and the six-inch to one-mile plan of the drop zone with all the hazards marked on it; these documents are essentially for your own protection as in the event of any CAA enquiry into that particular display these will support the actions you have initiated. Now you can carry out the other two essential pieces of paperwork. First, apply for any air traffic control clearance. The actual air traffic control clearance procedure is as follows:

1 Conditions of ATC clearance will be that the DZ must be clearly visible from the aircraft and that the aircraft maintains VMC. For display parachuting this means:

Outside controlled airspace at or below 3,000 ft amsl—clear of cloud, in sight of the surface and in a flight visibility of at least 3nm.

In controlled airspace or above 3,000 ft amsl—1nm horizontally and 1,000 ft vertically away from cloud and in a flight visibility of at least 5nm.

The above operating conditions should be made clear to those responsible for issuing any necessary air traffic clearance.

2 Locate the display drop zone *accurately* on the 1:500,000 aeronautical chart. In order of possibility it will be either:

(a) outside controlled airspace;
(b) inside controlled airspace;
(c) inside regulated airspace, e.g. SRA, SRZ, ATZ, MATZ or prohibited area, or restricted airspace, e.g. danger area.

3 Outside both controlled airspace and any SRA, SRZ, ATZ or MATZ air traffic clearance is not strictly necessary. For obvious safety reasons, however, even though the aircraft may be flying above a SRA, SRZ, ATZ or MATZ but the parachutists will drop through such airspace, liaison must be made with the appropriate ATC unit. Liaison with the appropriate ATC should also be made as follows:

(a) Up to 5nm from aerodrome traffic zone; telephone at least 7 days prior to the display. R/T communication throughout the display if required by the ATC unit. If no radio facility, a telephone call prior to take off.
(b) 5–10 nm away from any aerodrome traffic zone; telephone at least one day prior to the display. R/T or telephone communication as in (a) above.
(c) Up to 5nm from CTR, TMA, airway, SRA, SRZ or MATZ boundary. R/T communication throughout display if required by appropriate ATC unit.

4 Inside controlled airspace It is important that the various types of controlled airspace are thoroughly understood. They are as follows:

Control zone (CTR) extends from ground level to a given altitude or flight level.

Terminal control area (TMA) extends from a given altitude to a given flight level. It follows that there is uncontrolled airspace below a TMA and this may often be used freely for parachuting (as in para 3 above).

Airway (allocated a colour and number, e.g. Green 1) extends from a given altitude or flight level to a given flight level. Airspace below is uncontrolled as in the case of TMA above.

ATC clearance Initial contact should be made in writing with the relevant ATC authority as far in advance as possible and certainly not less than two weeks before the display. A personal visit arranged beforehand, or a telephone call, will do much to facilitate a greater understanding of the problems affecting both parties.

It is highly unlikely that *prior* clearance for the aircraft to drop parachutists from within an airway will be given. Clearance may well be available, however, on an opportunity basis by calling the airways controller on the relevant frequency at least 10 minutes before estimated entry, *but only* if the aircraft is transponder equipped. The display altitude should therefore be *planned* to be below airway level, and if penetration is in the event granted, this can be regarded as a bonus.

Air traffic clearance into controlled airspace is dependent upon two-way R/T communication, and, in the case of permanent IFR airspace, normally also the required navigational equipment and the pilot possessing a valid instrument rating.

5 SRA, SRZ, ATZ or MATZ Air traffic clearance is necessary from the aerodrome concerned. Whilst this is normally obtained by R/T before entry, in the case of parachute displays agreement in principle should be reached with the ATC concerned at the time the display is being planned; the following information is required:

(a) Date
(b) Time period

(c) Location of DZ
(d) Aircraft type and registration
(e) Aircraft operator
(f) Departure aerodrome
(g) Altitude required

It should be noted that some SRZs and ATZs are situated within controlled airspace. In these cases, air traffic clearance procedure is as described in para 4 above.

6 Prohibited areas These are annotated as 'P' on the aeronautical charts and flight or dropping within are definitely not permissible.

7 Danger areas *The UK Air Pilot* lists all danger areas which have an upper limit in excess of 500 ft above surface level. These are shown on the aeronautical charts, annotated 'D', and in the majority of cases are military ranges. They are not always active. Good airmanship requires that flights or drops within should only be made with the agreement of the range controlling authority.

8 Altimetry
Height is the vertical measurement from ground or aerodrome level datum and is termed QFE. It is used for parachutists' altimeters. This level appears on the aeronautical charts thus—300'. If associated with an amsl value (e.g. in regard to an obstruction thus—(300)).

Altitude is the vertical measurement from mean sea level datum and is termed QNH. It appears on the aeronautical charts thus—3500' ALT. If associated with a ground level value (e.g. in regard to an obstruction) thus—1200'.

Flight level is the vertical measurement using standard atmospheric pressure altimeter setting of 1013·2 millibars. It appears on the aeronautical charts thus—FL 55 (i.e. 5,500 ft).

9 Other display activities It must be remembered that parachuting may not be the only aviation activity at a particular show. Details of other such activities should be obtained from the organisers and liaison should be made accordingly, particularly with reference to a common R/T frequency.

Secondly, notify the Civil Aviation Authority of that particular display. Some may consider the next step unnecessary but the writing of an instruction for each display is a systematic way of ensuring everyone knows exactly what is planned. The instructions might well be produced under headings which provide a logical layout to cover all aspects as follows.

Instructions

1 Display
  (a) Title
  (b) Day/date
  (c) Time
  (d) Maps required
  (e) Organisers

2 Personnel
  (a) Team leader
  (b) Team
  (c) Commentator
  (d) DZ party (to include driver)

3 Aircraft
  (a) Type
  (b) Operators
  (c) Aircraft base
  (d) Mounting base
  (e) Frequencies

4 Programme: this should give all the timings from when the team meet before display to when the team line up after it.

5 DZ information
  (a) Brief description to include any particular hazards
  (b) DZ height and setting of altimeter at mounting airfield

6 Communications
  (a) Details of any radio you may be using
  (b) All useful telephone numbers: mounting airfield, aircraft base, showground

7 Administration
  (a) Vehicle
  (b) DZ equipment (to include target panels, smoke flares, anomometer, medical pack, etc.)
  (c) Dress (for team and DZ party)

These instructions should be sent

to all the personnel in section 2, the aircraft operators, the show organisers and any relevant air traffic control. When sending a copy to the latter include on it the display number if the show is subject to any air traffic clearance.

'Dirt-diving' an eight-way formation.

Team selection

The selection of your team needs careful consideration. The qualifications given earlier in this section can be misleading; for example a well-trained BPA C Certificate holder could easily be more reliable than a happy-go-lucky D Certificate holder. Naturally you are going to have to train beginners for displays so start them off on the easier display drop zones and have them positioned at the back of any group so that they can

123

follow the more experienced jumpers into the arena.

The equipment for the team usually consists of uniform jumpsuits (a well turned out team always creates a better impression than a bunch of scruffs in varying types of dress), plenty of wind drift indicators and smoke brackets. The latter should be designed with two independent means of securing them to the parachutist's foot, and team members should be constantly aware of the problems of jumping with smoke and the prime necessity for only setting them off *after* exit from the aircraft. Steerable reserve parachutes are strongly recommended for all members of teams regularly jumping into restricted drop zones. An air photo or large scale map of the drop zone will assist the jumpmaster in showing exit and opening points to the pilot and members of the team.

DZ party
The DZ party plays an important part in the display. Apart from being equipped with target panels and medical pack, smoke flares and an anomometer can give the team extra guidance. An anemometer, however, is useless unless it is both accurate and sited away from buildings, etc. where it can give a true reading. The DZ party should ideally be dressed the same as the team and must be carefully briefed

on their duties, which should include the signals for both temporarily halting the display and for cancelling it altogether should the wind speed exceed the pre-arranged limits (these may vary depending on the problems of each particular drop zone). Obviously in this connection a ground-to-air radio link can help the communication situation enormously.

Commentary
A good commentary always adds final polish to a good display and it is best if the team has its own commentator who knows each individual personally and who can *ad lib* with additional details if necessary. A commentator should always be interestingly factual and must resist the temptation to sensationalise the display by saying how incredibly dangerous it is and the like. If you have no regular commentator make sure a comprehensive commentary brief is sent to the organisers well in advance together with any photos of the team for publicity before the display.

Equipment
On the display day itself all equipment should be checked before moving off and, if possible, each member of the team should

have a look at the drop zone beforehand, now with its full car parks and bustling beer tents, etc. This is also a good time to set altimeters. After discussion with the organisers and final briefing of the DZ party the team should move to the emplaning airfield. Here the team leader can brief the pilot and the team together, having obtained the final meteorological report. The final met. report will give the jumpmaster an idea of whether the team will be reduced by cloud to giving a 'low' show, or if a 'high' show looks possible you will be able to obtain details of the upper winds for calculation of the freefall drift. Make sure you emplane and take off in plenty of time, having calculated the flying time from the mounting airfield to overhead the drop zone.

The programme
The exact programme of your display will be dependent upon the experience of your team members and the weather conditions on the day. Ideally your displays should be kept as simple as possible and often a simple display, slickly performed, will impress the crowd much more than a badly attempted piece of elaborate parachuting. As your team gains more experience the routine can be developed into something more elaborate, with either relative work or CRW being

parts of the routine.

The display can be cancelled by either the DZ party or the jumpmaster. The DZ party has to make its decision on the anemometer and the jumpmaster's decision will be a combination of his last minute met. check and the distance the wind drift indicator has travelled. If the last minute met. check is pessimistic, it is courteous to contact the show organisers and, having pointed out the possible outcome, ask them if they want you to fly, bearing in mind that they are paying for that flying time. Now a most important point which has already been made but it will do no harm to make it again: the decision of the drop zone party and/or jumpmaster must *never* be influenced by either the organiser's pleadings or by the desire not to disappoint a crowd no matter how many thousands they number. The pressures to carry out a display in marginal conditions can be substantial and must be resisted at all costs.

Once having decided to go, however, each member of the team should know both exit point and opening point. The experienced men should lead the less experienced into the arena but all team members must keep a good lookout around them, especially close to the ground. On landing, just be satisfied on achieving an into-wind landing in the arena; do not be tempted to make a precision accuracy approach to the cross which could result in injury in marginal conditions, and certainly will not impress anyone.

Once your team are on the ground it will round off the display tidily if you all line up for the crowd. The organisers might well like to take this opportunity to present their special guest visitor to the team and this is a detail that can be arranged beforehand. After your equipment is safely stowed away in your vehicle and you have signed the inevitable autograph or two, you can now enjoy whatever hospitality the organisers have arranged, assuming you have not got another display to perform that afternoon.

Finally, when you send the organisers the bill for your display, a covering letter saying thank you for their hospitality or whatever will go a long way towards their engaging you the following season. Always remember that a well performed display is not only very satisfying but it also benefits the sport as a whole. On the other hand, the press are very quick to pounce on a display that misfires and the subsequent bad publicity can be very damaging. Good planning and strict regard for safety will produce successful results.

19. Parachuting at night, into water and from high altitude

The three types of parachute descent described in this section are grouped together because they all tend to be undertaken only occasionally, are more elaborate in their planning and preparation, and special permission is required in each case from the Civil Aviation Authority. However, they are enjoyable facets of the sport and it is very satisfying to have them recorded in your log book.

Night parachute descents

Sport parachuting at night is not purely a question of jumping in reduced visibility, since there are additional problems resulting from reduced visibility: the extra equipment needed, the possibility of disorientation, a larger DZ party than usual and the need for a thorough briefing beforehand.

Parachuting at night is not covered in the normal permission issued by the Civil Aviation Authority and therefore special permission will have to be obtained in advance of a night jumping programme. In requesting this permission the Club Chief Instructor should send all details of the programme and the qualifications of those parachutists involved. Parachutists should have at least the equivalent of the BPA's C Certificates, and the planning and briefing should be undertaken by an instructor well acquainted with the procedures. The planning should include thorough familiarisation with the drop zone and its particular hazards, and it should be viewed at night to see the location of lights from houses, street lamps, etc. The pilot should obviously have a night rating on his licence and will be responsible for ensuring that the flying side is organised, with runway and aircraft lights operative, dimmed instrument lights and navigation lights working, etc. An experienced drop zone controller is required who should have working with him a team of reasonably experienced parachutists who will be required to ensure that those jumping are reached immediately after landing

in case of possible injury. There must also be a reporting procedure.

Extra equipment will be the types of lighting required. Each parachutist should have a torch strapped on the inside of one forearm pointing towards the hand; its purpose is to enable the jumper to see the reserve handle if necessary and, once his hands have located the steering toggles, the canopy itself will be lit which will help the DZ party to spot the jumper. Instruments should be lit with a shaded light and this should be red in colour so that night vision is not impaired. The third personal light is a bright orange or yellow light attached to the top of the jumper's helmet so that he can be readily seen from above, both in freefall and under the open canopy. Each of these three lights should be switched on just prior to exit, having been tested on the ground during the normal pre-jump checks. The target should be well illuminated and in a way that is easily recognisable. Five pressure lamps, each manned by a member of the DZ party, set in the centre of the cross and one on each extremity are as good a way as any.

If there are any prominent hazards on the drop zone these should also be made visible. Normally it is best to throw the wind drift indicator just before last light as a specially illuminated one is not

always very satisfactory. The pre-night jump briefing should involve the pilot, the DZ party and the jumpers and should cover the complete routine of each jump, emphasizing the need for every jumper in each lift to be accounted for before the next takes off. The jumpers should be reminded of the possibility of disorientation (especially on very dark nights), emergency procedures, canopy inspection and the necessity to protect night vision. The opening point should be clearly marked with a particular pattern of light which might well be two cars with their headlight beams at rightangles to one another.

During the descent the jumper should illuminate his canopy as much as possible to enable the DZ party to keep him in sight. Below about 200 ft the jumper should not rely on the altimeter but the odd glance at the lights on the DZ will give him a fair idea of his height. The set-up for the landing should be facing into wind and relaxed enough to take the unexpected landing. Having touched down safely the jumper should report immediately to the DZ controller to obviate unnecessary searches.

Gradual progression during night descents is imperative and the budding night jumper should not exceed more than 20 seconds on his first night jump. Relative work at night is feasible but should be approached with a good deal of caution. In conclusion the following four points on night vision are considered vital:

1 Smoking will adversely affect night vision and should not be indulged in for at least an hour before the jump.

2 Oxygen deficiency adversely affects night vision and starts to take effect soon after take off. This deficiency becomes dangerous above 8,000 ft.

3 Some parachutists naturally have poor night vision and should be dissuaded from parachuting at night.

4 Bright lights adversely affect night vision so beware of bright sunlight that day and photographers' flash bulbs; and the interior of buildings should be avoided for at least 30 minutes prior to take off. Final preparation should be done using red light as this does not affect night vision at all.

Your night jump will only be safely enjoyable if planned in detail, and this is also true of water and high altitude jumps.

Water descents

Intentional water descents provide yet another experience in the sport which is only dangerous when badly planned. As for night descents, water descents should be restricted to C or D (BPA) Certificate holders and the arrangements co-ordinated by an instructor. Once again the Civil Aviation Authority will have to issue a permission for a water jump programme as there are few expanses of water that are located within the boundaries of government or licensed airfields. The two golden rules of water descents are the provision and use of efficient life jackets, and the provision of a minimum of one power boat per parachutist on each load.

The preparation for the programme consists initially of dress and equipment for the parachutists. The dress is either an old pair of trousers and a shirt, or old jumpsuit with plimsolls. If there is any chance of a landing being made on dry land, a pair of basketball boots will provide a little more ankle support. Helmets are worn as usual. For competition water jumping by properly coached, experienced parachutists a swimming costume is all that need be worn. The life jacket is the most important piece of personal equipment; it should be small

enough to be worn under the parachute harness and should ideally be carbon dioxide operated. All life jackets should be checked for operation before use. You should also be aware of the danger of prematurely inflating the life jacket by accidental operation of the CO_2 bottle either in the aircraft or after exit, as the inflated life jacket will seriously restrict your movements. If an altimeter is used, some form of preventing its emersion in water must be devised; remember, it is no good putting it in a polythene bag and tying up the opening because the instrument is barometrically operated!

Preparation in the landing area consists of mooring the target, which may be any brightly coloured inflatable buoy, and the laying on of enough power boats for recovery. The DZ controller must be an experienced parachutist who is well aware of the particular problems involved. The pre-jump briefing should concern everyone involved, as with the night jump, but in water jumping the recovery by boat is probably the most critical feature. Having exited the aircraft the parachutist will not only be steering his parachute but also making ready for the landing by inflating the life jacket and either preparing to cut away the main canopy or to abandon the harness by undoing the chest strap and leg straps as described earlier. As you touch the water, you can either cut away or drop clear of your harness and wait to be picked up. Remember that once the canopy has become water-logged it will sink so try to grab a hold of it and hang on to it until the power boat arrives to pick you up.

The recovery should now go ahead as soon as you touch down with each boat moving towards its own previously nominated parachutist. Two points are worth mentioning: first, the danger of rigging line or canopy fouling the boat's propeller, and second, once an outboard motor is lifted clear of the water the boat has little or no means of steerage.

After jumping into salt water all your equipment must be carefully washed, using a weak soap powder solution, and thoroughly rinsed to avoid the risk of corrosion. Drying both the canopies is simply a matter of hanging them by the apex and allowing them to drip dry; packs and harnesses will inevitably take a little longer. Resist the temptation to hang them out in bright sunlight and don't be fooled into believing that the quickest way of drying a canopy is to jump it. If you should decide to carry this foolhardy idea through you will find that the deployment will take three to four times as long because of the extra weight that the pilot-chute has to lift

off your back. Therefore, make sure your equipment is thoroughly dry before you repack. A well-planned water descent is a refreshing diversion on a warm summer's day.

High altitude jumping

Parachutists are restricted by the Civil Aviation Authority to a maximum jump height of 12,000 ft above mean sea level without oxygen. Making descents from above 12,000 ft requires a good deal more planning and expensive equipment than water or night descents because of the many problems with which the parachutist is confronted. In Britain any parachutist wishing to make a high altitude descent is obliged to send his proposed plans and details of his equipment to the Safety and Training Committee of the British Parachute Association at least four weeks in advance for approval. For this reason I will only outline the problems for specialised advice is required on equipment and planning which the Safety and Training Committee will be able to arrange. If you are considering a high altitude descent a D Certificate (BPA) should for safety's sake be the absolute minimum required qualification.

Lack of oxygen causes a condition known as 'anoxia' which, if allowed to continue, will ultimately

result in unconsciousness. From 10,000 to 15,000 ft the individual is prone to drowziness and sluggishness; from 15,000 to 20,000 ft drowziness and sluggishness become more pronounced, thinking is slow and unreliable and vision tends to become blurred. From 20,000 to 25,000 ft loss of muscular control is apparent, corrective and protective actions are not possible and loss of consciousness will follow rapidly. If the individual is exposed to oxygen deficiency his time of useful consciousness is reduced with increase in altitude; for example, he will have 30 minutes of useful consciousness at 18,000 ft, 5 minutes at 22,000 ft and under a minute at 35,000 ft, with no more than 6 seconds at 65,000 ft. These symptoms of anoxia will vary with rate of ascent of the aircraft, length of exposure to oxygen, individual physical fitness and tolerance, amount of physical activity and the decrease in temperature. To simplify the oxygen requirement it is usual that supplementary oxygen is used in the aircraft until the moment of exit from heights between 12,000 and 20,000 ft; above 20,000 ft oxygen is used both in the aircraft (normally from a console) and in freefall (from a bail-out oxygen bottle of about 2 minutes duration).

Hyper-ventilation is another problem with which the high altitude

A water jump at the end of a World Championships.

jumper should be acquainted. Breathing involves inhaling life-giving oxygen and exhaling waste carbon dioxide. The provision of additional oxygen at high altitude by rapid breathing (or hyper-ventilation) simply does not work; instead it produces conditions of dizziness, spots before the eyes and numbness or tingling in fingers and toes which ultimately lead to unconsciousness. If the parachutist experiences these symptoms he may have been hyper-ventilating and the cure is simply to slow the rate of breathing deliberately or even to hold the breath for 10–15 seconds. If the symptoms then start to disappear it is a sure bet the jumper has been hyper-ventilating. The danger with both hyper-ventilation and anoxia is that the more one is exposed to either, the less one is mentally aware of one's actions.

At high altitude cold is extreme, remaining below 0°C above 20,000 ft the year round. As a rough guide temperature decreases 3·5°F for every thousand feet; this means that frost-bite is another potential problem for the high altitude parachutist.

Because of the thinner atmosphere at altitude (above 15,000 ft), terminal velocity is faster (less air resistence to the falling body). Turns and tracking become non-operative above 20,000 ft. The following table gives lengths of delays (with opening heights of 2,500 ft) above 12,000 ft:

Delay in seconds	Altitude
60	12,500 ft
65	13,500 ft
70	14,500 ft
75	15,500 ft
80	16,500 ft
85	17,500 ft
90	18,500 ft
95	20,000 ft

Delay in seconds	Altitude
125	25,000 ft
130	27,000 ft
135	29,000 ft
140	31,000 ft
175	35,000 ft
180	37,000 ft
190	40,000 ft
195	43,500 ft

Due to the problems associated with high altitude jumping it is an obvious requirement that barometric opening devices are used as an emergency back-up. It is because of the more costly nature of high altitude descents that they are undertaken the least frequently of the three types of parachuting discussed in this section.

20. Instructors and riggers

Instructors and riggers shoulder a heavy burden of responsibility, with the former literally taking the lives of his students during their training into his hands, while the latter's patient skill assures the safe operation of the parachutists' equipment. The thought of assuming these responsibilities will deter many from qualifying as instructors or riggers; therefore, qualifying as an instructor or rigger is most certainly not another stage in the parachuting progression.

Instructors should have a basic working knowledge of rigging and the qualities particularly required by sport parachute instructors could also apply to riggers; they are as follows:

1 The type of parachuting with which we are concerned is that which people do for enjoyment. That is why it is called sport parachuting, and the good instructor must realise this and do as little as possible to interfere with the enjoyment of the sport. He must, therefore, be *approachable*. There is a tendency among instructors to become less approachable when they gain more expertise and a position of greater stature within their club; this tendency towards aloofness should be strongly resisted as any student should feel completely at ease to approach his instructor with any query, however trivial it may seem. It is also worth the instructor casting his mind back to his own student days and remembering the difficulties with which he himself was faced; humility is, therefore, part of approachability.

2 The primary concern in all parachuting must always be safety. It almost goes without saying, but not quite, that the good instructor must be *safety-conscious*. In an effort to beat poor weather to get a student a jump, the less experienced instructor may be tempted to bend the rules. *This is irresponsible*. Any sport parachuting decision can nearly always be made correctly after asking yourself the question, 'Is it safe?'

3 Safety cannot be achieved without supervision and a willingness on the part of all concerned to stick to the rules, which is, of course, discipline.

To produce discipline an instructor must be *firm*. He will usually find it easier to be firm if he is also fair; in a student's natural enthusiasm to progress quickly he will appreciate the instructor's firm decision if the reason is explained to him fairly.

4 The good instructor, who is responsible for the safety of those in his care, should, therefore, be firm, but not overbearing. He must accept only the response and compliance under which safe parachuting can be conducted. He will, as in most other activities, achieve much by *good example*. The average student will always regard his instructor with a certain amount of awe and will inevitably tend to follow his example whether good or bad, or whether connected with parachuting itself or not. It is important that the student parachutist sees his instructor as an active parachutist himself.

5 Freefall parachuting is more than a skill. It requires a cool head, concentration and judgment, as well as body control and agility. In the early stages a novice is liable to feel a little apprehensive. The instructor can help him to overcome this by imparting *confidence*. There is only one thing worse in this respect than a lack of confidence, and that is over-confidence. The latter leads to acceptance of risks which in turn inevitably results in accidents. An over-confident parachutist is a menace to himself and to others; he should be supervised closely and if necessary suspended.

6 Parachuting can be a complex matter and the supervision of it more so. The instructor carries a good deal of responsibility and has much to think about. He cannot, for example, instruct others if his mind is on his own parachuting. When he is instructing he must concentrate wholly on his instruction. To ensure that nothing is overlooked, he must be *systematic*.

7 When conditions are right for parachuting there is a tendency for people to become impatient. Haste leads to danger, because sooner or later something important is overlooked. 'If you are in a hurry, you are in danger' is a good parachuting motto. The good instructor must, therefore, be *alert but unhurried*.

8 Parachuting is not always straightforward. Many parachutists experience problems sooner or later. Most of them are minor, but at the time they are cause for concern. Often the parachutist cannot determine the reasons for his problems and it is up to the instructor to spot them for him and explain how they can be overcome. For this reason he must be *observant*. There is a good deal of skill in being able to spot the student's mistakes and then deliver a clear critique to him afterwards. It is a skill which develops with practice but its importance cannot be stressed enough for the student is wasting his jump if he is not learning from it.

9 There is no substitute for practical experience. The highly experienced is better than the less experienced because he has personally met and overcome many of the problems which from time to time will confront his pupils. But no instructor, however expert, will ever experience all the problems of others. He will, on the other hand, often be called upon to give advice, and to do so he must understand parachuting in all its aspects; this can only be achieved through intensive study and intelligent discussions. To this end he must have an *enquiring mind*.

10 Only a limited proportion of capable parachutists make good instructors. They often lack one or more of the qualities referred to above. Even if they have them all there is yet another which is as important as any of the others. In accepting his responsibilities a parachute instructor is entrusted with the lives of other people. This he must never for a second forget. He must never take a chance or run a risk, however small, in case the outside chance comes up. To avoid the acceptance of risks he must in the first place recognise them as such and, in order to achieve the standard of knowledge which this demands, he must be dedicated to his responsibilities. Until, therefore, he has a *sound knowledge* of all aspects of the sport, combined with considerable practical experience, energy, enthusiasm and the ability to instruct, he should not put himself forward to his club chief instructor for a recommendation to attend an instructor's course.

Skydiving photographs are so visually exciting that they are often used as a promotional medium—in this case for pork pies.

Appendix: Extracts from BPA Operations Manual

Conduct and Control of Sport Parachuting

The Ten Basic Rules

1.   All parachuting within BPA Affiliated Clubs, Schools, Centres and Associations must take place under the following conditions:

(1)   Under arrangements made by a BPA Advanced Instructor who has been nominated as the Club Chief Instructor (CCI) and who is normally present when parachuting is in progress.

(2)   By parachutists who are in every respect fit, trained, dressed, equipped and briefed to undertake the descent planned.

(3)   When an adequate ground control organisation is in operation.

(4)   With an approved pilot, and a jumpmaster qualified to dispatch the parachutists concerned.

(5)   With parachutes in good condition, safe in all respects, correctly packed, well fitted, and inspected before emplaning.

(6)   From an authorised type of aircraft suitably equipped and prepared for parachuting.

(7)   When weather conditions are suitable.

(8)   Onto an approved DZ.

(9)   With all documentation in order and up to date.

(10)   According to the conditions laid down in the BPA Operations Manual.

2.   Responsibility

(a)   Overall responsibility within BPA Affiliated Clubs, Schools, Centres and Associations for ensuring that the conditions enumerated in Paragraph 1 above are observed, will be vested in Club Chief Instructors (CCIs).

(b)   Student Parachutists (see Section 2) may only parachute under the organised control of a BPA Affiliated Club, School or Centre and under the supervision of a CCI or BPA Instructor authorised by a CCI. Such instructors will be wholly responsible for their training and parachuting activities.

3.   Ground Control Organisation

All Clubs, Schools and Centres will establish a satisfactory system of Ground Control to control parachuting which must be continuously operational when parachuting is in progress and which will meet the following minimum requirements.

(1)   All parachutists must be briefed and inspected before emplaning.

(2)   All aircraft lifts must be correctly manifested before take off.

(3)   DZ Control must be continuously established when parachuting is in progress, and the descent of all parachutists must be monitored from the ground.

(4)   Parachutists under instruction must be debriefed after every descent.

(5)   Parachutists' log books and other relevant records must be maintained up to date.

(6)   Parachute packing by all those who do not possess a Parachute Packing Certificate must be adequately supervised.

4.   Briefing of Parachutists before Emplaning

(a)   All Parachutists under instruction must be briefed by a CCI (or an instructor nominated by him) on the details of every planned descent before parachutes are fitted.

(b)   All other parachutists will notify the type of jump they propose to carry out to the instructor or J/M who is compiling the manifest, together with all relevant details. This will enable the J/M to complete the briefing of the entire lift.

5.   Manifesting of Parachutists

All Parachutists must be manifested on a form designed for the purpose before emplaning. It is normally desirable for the J/M to carry a copy in the aircraft. It is essential that one copy is left in the hands of a responsible member of the Ground Control Staff. It is recommended that all Clubs should use a Manifest Board on which the names of the parachutists in every planned aircraft lift should be displayed where it can be read by all concerned.

6. D.Z. Control

(a)   A Control organisation must be set up on all DZs to ensure that parachuting is safely and efficiently controlled at all times. It should be fully established by the time each lift takes off and must remain in force until all parachutists (and aircraft if applicable) have landed.

(b)   The DZ Controller must be a responsible parachutist who has been fully briefed on his duties by the CCI. Except in the case of Display Team where the DZ Controller may be a responsible persón, nominated by the Team Leader.

(c)   The duties of a DZ Controller may be varied as necessary in order to fit in with local conditions provided that the safety standards which they are intended to achieve are in no way reduced.

(d)   The DZ Controller may be assisted by any number of others but he/she alone is responsible for ensuring ground control is fully established and that all the functions allocated to him/her are efficiently carried out. When parachuting is in progress his/her correct place is normally either at the target or at a control post. He/she must ensure that all parachute landings on the DZ are monitored.

(e)   The recommended duties of a DZ Controller are that he/she:

(1)   Will be responsible for setting up and supervising the DZ Control Organisation as required by the CCI.

(2)   Will be given clear instructions from the CCI on the extent, if any, to which he is responsible for the briefing and supervision of marshallers, J/Ms and parachutists.

(3)   Must ensure that the pilot's briefing includes any DZ Control Instructions or Information which is of concern to them.

(4)   Will brief any assistants of staff who are placed at his disposal or who are in any way made responsible to him by the CCI.

(5)   Must lay out the target at the point indicated by the CCI.

(6)   Must display the appropriate ground to air signals for the guidance of the Pilot and J/M when necessary.

(7)   Must set up and maintain watch on a wind meter, or be in communication with someone who holds this responsibility.

(8)   Must ensure that the target area is clear of parked vehicles, etc.

(9)   Must ensure that a stretcher and First Aid Kit are at all times available and that someone with First Aid knowledge is known to him. He should also know the most direct route to the nearest hospital.

(10)   Must prevent large groups of spectators from approaching too close to the target area.

(11)   Will maintain a close look out for aircraft including gliders, and will suspend parachuting as soon as any interference with the safe conduct of parachuting becomes apparent.

(12)   Will keep a close watch on wind and weather and suspend parachuting if either should exceed or threaten to exceed the limits laid down.

(13)   Will ensure that all apparatus for wind indication on the DZ is put to proper use and the attention of the CCI drawn to any equipment which is lacking or unserviceable (wind socks, signal panels, smoke generators, etc.)

(14)   Will keep in close touch with Flying Control if there are other aviation activities adjacent to the DZ.

(15)   Will maintain radio communication with the parachuting aircraft if it is provided.

(16)   Must ensure that all parachutists' descents are observed, preferably through telemeters or binoculars, until all parachutists have landed.

(17)   Will ensure that all landed parachutists who are in need of assistance receive it without delay.

(18)   Will report all accidents,

injuries, parachute malfunctions and contraventions of BPA Operations Manual and Club Rules to the CCI.

7. Debriefing of Parachutists

All Parachutists under instruction should be debriefed after every descent. This should be in two parts: firstly on the exit by the instructor who acted as J/M and secondly, by the DZ Controller who observed the opening, canopy control and landing. The free fall should also be observed and noted either from the air or from the ground.

8. Parachute Packing

Arrangements for the supervision of parachute packing by all who do not possess a packing certificate must be planned in detail and understood by all concerned. Clubs may use their own systems providing that:

(a)   A holder of a packing certificate covering all types of parachutes likely to be packed in the packing area is nominated by the CCI to take charge of the packing area.

(b)   All parachutes are checked for damage after use and withdrawn if found unserviceable.

(c)   All parachutes are correctly packed. They must be checked at the appropriate stages by the packing certificate holder as qualified in sub para (a) above.

9. Ground to Air Signals

(a)   There will be a standard code of ground-to-air signals used by all BPA Affiliated Clubs, Schools and Centres. These will consist of red, orange, yellow or white panels of sufficient dimensions to be clearly visible by parachutists from whatever height they are jumping.

(b)   On the DZ there will be a target cross indicating the area which it is intended that parachutists will land and will be displayed whenever parachuting is in progress.

(c)   If radio communication is not used or there has been a breakdown of radio communication the following signals must be used.

(1)   The basic signal will be a cross (X) indicating the target in the vicinity of which it is intended that parachutists will land.

(2)   When the FULL CROSS (X) is displayed it indicates that conditions are judged to be safe for all Categories of Parachutists.

(3)   When the (X) is changed to a (T) it indicates that conditions are NOT suitable for all parachutists. Thereafter only parachutists authorised by the Chief Instructor may jump.

(4)   When the (X) or (T) is changed to an (I) this will indicate that all parachuting is temporarily suspended but the aircraft may remain airborne at the discretion of the pilot pending a further change of signals.

(5)   When (X), (T) or (I) is changed to (L) it will indicate to the pilot and jumpmaster that parachuting is suspended and the aircraft must LAND with all remaining parachutists on board.

(d)   Every DZ will be equipped with a windsock or other suitable means of conveying the strength and direction of wind to parachutists who are preparing to land.

The launch of a 4-way formation from a
BN2 Islander.

British Parachute Association Ltd.

Kimberley House 47 Vaughan Way Leicester LE1 4SG

Telephone: 59635/59778

PACKING CERTIFICATE

This is to certify that ....

Address ....

....

....

BPA No. ....

has been tested to the following standards :

1) Has reassembled a parachute assembly stripped down to the following components.
   a) Container and harness.
   b) Canopy and risers (or connector links).
   c) Pilot chute.
   d) Bridle cord.
   e) Sleeve and retaining line (if applicable).

2) Has successfully cleared the canopy/lines of twists and tangles.

3) Has performed a line sequence check.

4) Knows how to perform all the packing checks at the appropriate stages.

5) Has packed the parachute ready for jumping.

6) Has been instructed on how to inspect the assembly for damage and deterioration.

Name (BLOCK CAPITALS) .... *Instructor/Rigger

BPA No. ....

Signed .... FAI No. ....

BPA OFFICE USE ONLY

Date of issue ....

Docs. checked ....

Approved on behalf of BPA ....

Instructors/Riggers Please Note :

Once the conditions above have been complied with this form should be sent to the BPA for recording. Once it has been returned the specific types of assembly that the holder is cleared for should be listed overleaf. Any Instructor or Rigger may subsequently endorse this certificate for additional types without further reference to the BPA.

* Delete as appropriate.

The holder of this certificate (named overleaf) is cleared to pack the following specified parachute canopies and deployment devices into the following containers.

Canopy Type	Deployment Device	Container	Instructor's Signature	BPA No.	FAI No.	Date

N.B. Deployment devices include static line mouthlock bags, static line centre base tie bags, sleeves, diapers, multilock diapers, etc. The column headed 'Container' should include type and manufacturer. If this is not known then give brief description (e.g. 'one pin student main' or 'two pin wonderhog type reserve').

British Parachute Association Packing Certificate.

Air traffic clearance must be confirmed
before every parachute display.

 British Parachute Association Ltd.

Kimberley House 47 Vaughan Way Leicester LE1 4SG
Telephone: 59635/59778

REQUEST FOR AIR TRAFFIC CLEARANCE
FOR PARACHUTE DISPLAYS

The information below is required by the relevant ATC authority.

Reference BPA Registered Display Team No. ....

Address and Telephone No. of Team Leader ....

....

....

....

Display Team : ....

Date : ....

Time Period : ....

Aircraft operator : ....

Location of DZ : ....

....

Co-ordinates (Grid Reference) : ....

Proposed dropping height : ....

Type of Aircraft and Registration Letters : ....

Departure Aerodrome : ....

Signature..

Date ....

The ATC provisional clearance information will be recorded below.

Parachute Display Number : ....

ATC Instructions to operator : ....

Frequencies to be carried : ....

Signed :.. Telephone No. and Extension : ....

Date : ....

ATC Unit : ....

Address of requests for Controlled Airspace Clearance:

LONDON
ATC (Ops) 1,
London Air Traffic Control
Centre,
Porter Way,
West Drayton,
Middlesex.

Tel: 08954 44077 Ext. 2229

MANCHESTER
Manchester ATC Sub Centre
(Ops 1),
Manchester International
Airport,
Wythenshawe,
Manchester,
M22 5PB

Tel: 061 499 5313 (Weekdays)
061 499 5320 (Sat/Sun)

BIRMINGHAM
Birmingham ATC Watch
Supervisor,
Birmingham International
Airport,
Elmdon,
Birmingham,
B26 3QN

Tel: 021 743 6227

Index

Numbers in italics refer to illustration captions

A British 8-way team in transition.